CREATIVE
ECOLOGIES

CREATIVE ECOLOGIES

Where Thinking Is a Proper Job

John Howkins

Transaction Publishers
New Brunswick (U.S.A.) and London (U.K.)

First Transaction publication 2010
Copyright © 2009 by John Howkins.

This book is printed on acid-free paper that meets the American National Standard for Permanence of Paper for Printed Library Materials.

Library of Congress Catalog Number: 2010012584
ISBN: 978-1-4128-1428-7
Printed in the United States of America

Library of Congress Cataloging-in-Publication Data

Howkins, John, 1945-
    Creative ecologies : where thinking is a proper job / John Howkins.
        p. cm.
    Originally published: St Lucia, Qld. : University of Queensland Press, 2009.
    Includes bibliographical references and index.
    ISBN 978-1-4128-1428-7
    1. Creative ability in business. 2. Economics. 3. Success in business.
    I. Title.

HD53.H69 2010
650.1'3--dc22

2010012584

Contents

Introduction

The main question of our age is how we live our lives. As we struggle with this, we face other questions. How do we handle ideas and knowledge, both our own and other people's? What relationship to ideas do we want? Whose ideas do we want to be surrounded by? *Where* do we want to think?

For young people, choosing their first job means choosing where to live: where to work, to meet people, to learn, to make friends. It is the first of many crossroads, as nowadays we change our communities and networks throughout our lives. Most of us choose, or have the choice made for us, according to what family, colleagues and friends do and say and what we read about, and a more or less rational calculation of the odds. We want to go where we can have fun, meet interesting people and make some money.

Every day, more people gain more freedom to make their

own choices about where to live and what to think. These modern-day nomads are so numerous that general principles are emerging, framed by history, sociology, geography, environmental studies, epidemiology, urban studies, ecology and demographics. We move, cities change their shape, social structures evolve, we adapt. People and companies move to be near each other. Property owners invest in urban regeneration. Governments draw up regional plans. Travel is the world's biggest industry, generating 10 per cent of the global economy.

Everyone makes a different choice. Our creativity is personal and private, and our ability to use it is variable and unreliable. It helps if you are in the right place at the right time. The old question 'Where do you want to live?' is now 'Where do you want to *think?*'

Ecology is the study of organisms and their environment, asking 'Why this?' 'Why here?' It tells us how organisms relate to each other through mimicry, symbiosis, collaboration and competition. It is holistic and radical and provocative, summoning evidence from human behaviour in cities, beetles in the desert and swarming bees to illustrate general rules on diversity, change, learning and adaptation.

Yet though we have Gregory Bateson's ecology of mind, Arne Naess's ecology of wisdom and many explorations of urban ecologies and network ecologies, attempts to use ecology to illuminate creativity have hardly begun, beyond using it as a fancy word for context. This is a pity, given the richness of both concepts. Ecology may help us to understand why thinking for oneself is treated as normal in some places but odd and antisocial in others.

Modern ecology is part of the shift in thinking generated by quantum physics and systems theory, from the old view based on reductionism, mechanics and fixed quantities to a new view based on holistic systems where qualities are contingent on the observer and on each other. This perception changes how people treat ideas and facts, certainties and uncertainties, and affects both art and science. Worldwide it is part of the process of understanding the current crisis in the natural environment and capitalism, and the balance of creativity and control required in our response.

This short book is an attempt to identify an ecology of thinking and learning. We need to escape from old, industrial ways and become more attuned to how people actually borrow, develop and share ideas. The assumption that everyone should be a full-time employee is old-fashioned industrialist ideology. Creative ecologies allow everybody to have a go.

Throughout, I have tried to ask questions and offer signposts. I give no guarantee that creative ecologies will be sustainable. But we should know what to aim for.

The Plan

The book's starting point is the increasing role that information has played in industrial economies since the 1800s and especially in the last thirty years. 'The Challenge' is how to integrate our current ideas about creativity into our understanding of information. Chapter 2, 'First Ideas', sketches the evolution of the phrase 'creative economy', concluding that conventional thinking is helpful but does not fully explain what is happening. It is too fragmented; we need a systems approach. Chapter 3, 'Scope and Scale', suggests that today's creative economies differ from previous systems in scope (they cover more activities) and scale (they involve more people).

Chapter 4, 'The Adaptive Mind', shows how the science of ecology clarifies the relationship between people's creativity and their environment. It describes the niches where creative people thrive. Creativity is not a matter of exceptional artistic talent or cultural riches but a rich mix of ecological factors, primarily diversity, change, learning and adaptation. It exists only where the ecology permits, and it flourishes through adaptive efficiency. Chapter 5, 'Creative Places', examines self-organising systems, cities and cyberspace. Chapter 6, 'Negotiating Uncertainty', examines how people navigate and negotiate in a creative ecology.

Chapter 7, 'The Way Forward', looks at growth models: growth being seen as an increase in learning capacity and adaptive behaviour. In the past, the fastest-growing ecologies have had the highest levels of freedom. Some governments welcome creative ecologies as the most efficient way of integrating people into local development processes, but others fear them for the same reason. Chapter 8, 'New Places, New Policies', explains why governments stuck within the framework of an industrial society have problems relating to a creative ecology.

Chapter 9, 'Three Steps to Growth', summarises the three principles of a creative ecology: first, the individual mind ('everyone is creative'), second, freedom ('creativity needs freedom'), and third, markets ('freedom needs markets').

Chapter 10, 'The New Billion', looks at the people who are

looking for their first job and seeking creative ecologies, both physical and online, for personal learning, work and growth.

Creative or Repetitive?

Throughout the book I refer to creative and repetitive systems with the following characteristics:

Creativity	*Repetition*
Diverse/variegated	Unified
Implicit	Explicit
Unstable (challenges/questions)	Stable (safe/answers)
Fluid/emerging	Rigid/settled
Feedback	Little feedback
Learning	Education
Networks	Hierarchies
Desires beauty	Desires order
Access	Control
High autonomy/low dependence	High dependence/low autonomy
Complex	Simple
Self-organising	Closed, shielded
Quality	Quantity
Systemic/whole	Fragmented/parts
Analogue	Digital (especially binary)
Cyclical	Linear
Process/collaboration	Event/competition
Mind	Body

1

The Challenge

Learning to Look

Being creative isn't easy. It cannot be taught, although it can be learned. Everyone has to learn the rules before they can break them. The best way to learn is to work with people who are better, wiser, than oneself, with people who are challenging and have the knack of picking the right challenges. With some activities, you want other people to be less talented or successful so you can get ahead; in the creative ecology, you want to work with people who are better than you so you can get ahead.

Read this letter from a 21-year-old man who was living in London in 1874 and working as a junior assistant in an art gallery. It was the end of a cold January day. He had finished the stocktaking and had enlivened a tedious job by looking hard at the pictures:

Admire as much as you can; most people don't admire enough. The following are some of the painters whom I like especially: Scheffer, Delaroche, Hebert, Hamon, Leys, Tissot, Lagye, Boughton, Millais, Thijs Maris, De Groux, De Braekeleer Jr, Millet, Jules Breton, Feyen-Perrin, Eugene Feyen, Brion, Jundt, George Saal, Israels, Anker, Knaus, Vautier, Jourdan, Compte-Calix, Rochussen, Meissonier, Madrazo, Ziem, Boudin, Gerome, Fromentin, Decamps, Bonington, Diaz, Th Rousseau, Troyon, Dupre, Corot, Paul Huet, Jacque, Otto Weber, Daubigny, Bernier, Emile Breton, Chenu . . .'[1]

Few people today could name so many painters. Was he exaggerating? I do not think so.

He had thought of being a commercial illustrator but doubted he could draw. His brother was keen, but his sister advised, 'Be a baker, that's a useful trade'. He started to copy other paintings and to illustrate his letters.

Nearly ten years later, thinking back on his decision to paint, he wrote to his brother:

> At the time when you spoke of my becoming a painter, I thought it very impractical and would not hear of it. What made me stop doubting was reading a clear book on perspective, Cassange's 'Guide to the ABC of Drawing', and a week later I drew the interior of the kitchen with stove, chair, table and window - in their places and on their right legs.[2]

All his life he roamed around Europe, living off family and friends, searching for the right place to work. He dreamed of a community of artists and, after many anxious letters, at last persuaded Paul Gauguin, an older and more successful painter, to stay in his little house in Arles. Their world consisted of the house, the countryside where they painted, the grocery, several bars and a brothel. They gave each other confidence - 'Look, here's someone else as crazy as I am' - practical advice, and a glimpse of a perfect life together.

Vincent Van Gogh's nine weeks with Gauguin in his studio were astonishingly creative for both of them. Van Gogh produced forty-nine oil paintings, several watercolours and hundreds of drawings and Gauguin about one-third as many. The Yellow House with its yellow furniture was an oasis for two nomads. It didn't last, but it was extraordinary while it did. By December, Van Gogh had started his voyage into madness and Gauguin returned to Paris and then to Martinique where he painted, at the end of his life, a canvas titled *Where Do We Come From? What Are We? Where Are We Going?*.

The buzz of hard work done well is exhilarating for those doing it and also for those who (are allowed to) watch. It is best when someone takes risks, and lets you see why and how. There is no better preparation or talisman for one's own journey. Like all creative activities, art is dependent upon novelty, but we only recognise novelty if we know what everyone else has already done, as Van Gogh appreciated on that dark January day in London. This is why creative people want to immerse themselves in other people's excitement and passions; to share their failures and successes; to get close.

Definitions

To begin, we need to differentiate between *creativity* and *creative economy*. *Creativity* is the use of ideas to produce new ideas. The input, the original idea, may be novel or familiar.

What is more important is that we use energy to transform it into novel outcomes. The output's commercial value may depend on its *uniqueness* (as with Van Gogh's paintings) or on how easily it can be *copied* (as with this book).

Creativity is a neuro-physical process that comes with a mix of emotions that add greatly to the pleasure, the kick, of thinking for oneself. It can be described but not defined and indeed has always been conditional. Ancient religions ascribe creativity to God and attribute Creation to a single Creator. In Europe up to the seventeenth century a Christian who claimed to be the sole source of his or her own ideas was regarded as blasphemous. Historically, Christians believed that God created the world (surveys indicate that about one-third of Americans still believe this). Islam describes Allah as the Creator and forbids representations of Allah or the Prophet.

Secular societies are no better guarantors of freedom and many regard independent thought with suspicion. In the fifth century BC, Plato lived his life on the basis of thinking for himself, but he banned artists from Utopia because he believed they would be disruptive. He was right. Today, totalitarian societies feel uncomfortable with free speech and forbid it. Every society, even the freest, places restrictions on what people can say and write and represent in images.

This raw creativity is not the same as talent, which is a kind of expertise, usually learned and repeatable. Nor is it the same as art, a tricky word, which refers both to particular kinds of expression and formats and to something done well. The argument rages whether there are any absolute standards in art (or beauty) or whether they are eternally relative. Since many brilliant minds have failed to resolve the dispute, the latter case is more likely to be true.[3]

Creativity is not the same as *innovation*. Creativity is internal, personal and subjective, whereas innovation is external and objective. Creativity often leads to innovation, but innovation seldom leads to creativity. Each creative domain tends to one or the other. Where success depends on personal expression, people want to be creative; if it depends on calculation and implementation they aim for innovation. Art for art's sake is fine, and has produced great work, but 'innovation for innovation's sake' is a waste of money.

Economy initially referred to the efficient management of a household or farm and then to the complex of human activities involved in production, spending, consumption and saving. Its base is the tension between what we want and what we can get, whether by producing our own goods and services or by buying someone else's. The economic conundrum presented by John Stuart Mill has been that, whereas our desires, wants and needs are infinite or at least indefinitely large, our resources are limited. We therefore have to make choices that affect our wealth and welfare, the market, and our future desires.

The way economics and business has approached this for the past fifty years has been to focus on one-off innovation implemented in mass production with ever lower costs and prices. Business has seen creativity and innovation as specialist functions. I call this the *repetitive economy*. We are now seeing a shift to the *creative economy* where, although basic goods and services have not diminished in absolute terms, the bulk of growth comes from their added symbolic value. Like other economic systems, the function of a creative economy is to use resources so as to increase wealth and welfare. But, while the commodities and manufactured goods in a classical economy are physical and quantifiable, the inputs and outputs of a creative economy are subjective and qualitative. The value of a commodity like a potato is its physical importance as food; and one potato is much like another. But the value of what I create is what it means to me and, possibly, what it means to others; and meanings are unstable.

Ecology is the study of relationships between organisms and their environment, which probably includes other organisms. An *eco-system* is an ecology of several different species living together. Scientists talk of *habitats,* which are real places like streams and urban environments, and also of *niches,* which are systems wherein a species thrives. Early ecologists worked in wild places, but nowadays they look more at managed eco-systems and niches. Cultivated eco-systems are the best model for human ecologies. Eco-literate models do not just 'let nature go', leaving it wild, nor are they exclusively centred on human interventions. They 'involve taking nature as its base and working with it to achieve your aims'.[4] *Deep ecology* eschews a human bias and takes nature's viewpoint.

A *creative ecology* is a niche where diverse individuals express themselves in a systemic and adaptive way, using ideas to produce new ideas; and where others support this endeavour even if they don't understand it. These energy-expressive relationships are found in both physical places and intangible communities; it is the relationships and actions that count, not the infrastructure. The strength of a creative ecology can be measured by these flows of energy and the continual learning and creation of meaning. The quartet of diversity, change, learning and adaptation mutually enhance each other.

I often refer to *self-organising systems,* which can be defined as systems whose internal dynamics lead to increases in complexity and stability without external guidance, and to *emergent* behaviour which is observed when a system, rather than its parts, causes a new pattern. Both terms originated in physics, but they exist in biology, in the ways birds flock together and bees swarm, in ecology, with deep ecology and the Gaia theory, and in sociology, with memes, of which more later.

The Origins of an Idea

There have been peaks of extraordinary thinking and inventiveness throughout human history, often linked to trade and empires. With hindsight, we can see that the peaks tend to be brief. Cultures emerge to provide a high-energy nutrient for creative achievement but seldom sustain it: Mesopotamia and Sumeria (the Fertile Crescent), Classical Greece, China in the Han Dynasty and later as well as today, Italy during the Roman Empire and again during the Renaissance in the fourteenth and fifteenth centuries, Arab science and civilisation in the ninth to eleventh centuries, and so on. It is invidious to make a list because so many cultures have flourished in ways we scarcely appreciate.

The origins of Western creativity can be traced back to the Renaissance of Greek and Roman classical ideas and to the birth of humanism. Europe has been astonishingly creative in philosophy, art and industry, flowering in culture continuously since the fifteenth century and in technology since the eighteenth. The Enlightenment upheld the claims of reason over doctrine (and sometimes of personal passion as a motor of reason) and provided an environment for independent expression, debate, the rule of law, the freedom of the press, accountable government, and independent public institutions. Although some believed it would lead to the death of religion, it did not do so, as Darwin discovered when he presented his ideas on the 'origin of species' in the 1860s.

The capital cities of London, Paris, Amsterdam, Rome, Berlin, Prague, Vienna and Moscow were world centres of creativity, invention and novelty (I call them *mini-ecologies*). New York, Chicago, Los Angeles and other American cities soon joined them. Some American scientists believe that the ecology of the Native American could not have developed civilisation and industry on its own and needed an injection of northern European values.[5] Once injected, and given the immigrants' commitment to freedom and entrepreneurship, America developed quickly to take a lead.

The first few decades of the twentieth century saw astonishing artistic, scientific and technological outbursts. Freud published his *Interpretation of Dreams* in 1900, Einstein published his theory of relativity five years later, and by the 1920s scientists realised that the Cartesian and Newtonian assumptions that matter consists of hard-edged things that could be objectified had been replaced with patterns of probabilities. These decades saw a tectonic shift in our handling of ideas, summed up in the new theories of quantum physics, from the old world view based on reductionism, mechanics and fixed quantities to a view based on holistic systems where qualities were contingent on the observer and on each other.

Originating in physics, these new perceptions had profound effects on all science and art and indeed on how people treat ideas and facts, certainties and uncertainties. We can trace modern creativity as a mass movement back to quantum physics and its implications for uncertainty, contingency and interdependence.

The Lumiere brothers had invented cinematography in 1896 and Picasso remade painting in his *Demoiselles D'Avignon* in 1907, followed by his experiments with African tribal art and cubism. Marcel Duchamp, who like Picasso was influenced by the French mathematician Henri Poincare, painted his *Nude Descending a Staircase* in 1912 and exhibited his even more controversial *Urinal* in New York in 1917. James Joyce wrote *Finnegan's Wake,* incidentally referring to Einstein as Winestain, and then 1922 saw both Joyce's *Ulysses* and T.S. Eliot's *The Waste Land.* Nijinsky invented a new choreography. The premiere of Stravinsky's *Rite of Spring* in 1913 caused a riot in Paris, only for Arnold Schoenberg to revolutionise music again a few years later with his *Pierrot Ensemble.* Marconi was developing radio and Louis Bleriot flew across the English Channel. The Dutch de Stijl, the German Bauhaus and the Russian School of Art and Design launched modern design and constructivism. It was the time of cabaret, cocktails, the Jazz Age, cinema and Dada. Technological innovation proliferated: safety razors, the latex condom, vacuum cleaners, air-conditioning, neon lights, windscreen wipers, bakelite, cellophane, instant coffee, stainless steel, the bra, the zip, pop-up toasters and frozen food.

The American Dream Machine

America was the first country in modern times to conjoin the arts and business and so practically invent popular culture, the notion that artists, the people and big business could speak the same language and enjoy the same pleasures. This is why, although the French invented cinematography, the Americans invented the movie business. It is evident in the work of Norman Rockwell, Walt Disney and Motown Records and most notably the internet. While many in Europe were shoring up ideological barriers between art and commerce, America found great delight in bundling them together and making money out of the cocktail. It is famous for its historic cultural and political freedoms, enshrined in the Constitution, and its robust competitiveness. It has been criticised for being too commercial, though these comments have been muted recently, and it was home to some of the most imaginative twentieth-century art, fiction, poetry, film, TV, music, fashion and architecture and has a rare ability to make designs and tell stories that appeal worldwide. Its social networks produce an extraordinary variety of emergent thinking.

Throughout the century, America, Europe and later Japan embarked on a spree of discovery, invention and innovation. Business became more competitive by reducing costs and expanding internationally. America shifted its focus from manufacturing to services, as did Europe, with only Germany, which has a worldwide reputation for technical R&D, maintaining a significant world-class manufacturing sector. In Britain, manufacturing declined precipitously and contributed only 14 per cent to GDP by 2007. At the same time, Britain's service sectors, especially finance, media and telecommunications, expanded quickly. Throughout Europe, each generation saw a further shift to these services. Western governments were enthusiastic because the alternative was unemployment. I described this change in *The Creative Economy:*

> On the supply side, automation in manufacturing industries and, to a smaller extent, in the service industries has cut the demand for manual labour, so young people are looking elsewhere for work. Many turn to the creative industries which offer an attractive lifestyle and above-average economic rewards. Market economies are skilful at meeting consumer needs, especially in the field of entertainment where consumer needs are so passionate and evanescent. Suppliers have become adept at charging for pleasure.[6]

Since then, these trends have become more pronounced. In 2007, Will Hutton, Director of the British Work Foundation, said, 'The trends behind this phenomenon - rich, discerning consumers seeking cultural satisfaction, and multiple businesses aiming to supply it, often using new technologies - are likely to grow'. In most European cities, about 50 per cent of workers work in so-called 'knowledge industries' and about 10 per cent in creative industries.

Manufacturing costs have fallen in absolute terms and as a proportion of total cost, while the costs of services such as design, branding, marketing, advertising, licensing, distribution and retailing have increased. Head offices now focus on owning brands and contract-out or off-shore their factories. This restructuring has shifted value chains. Companies still want lower costs and higher productivity but their chief targets are elsewhere. Upstream, design has become more important;

while downstream services now take between 50 per cent and 80 per cent of total costs.

The results are obvious on every High Street. By the 1980s, the process of buying had become as important as the thing bought, offering people multiple opportunities to express their own personality and to share in other people's personalities. People want to be similar to some people and dissimilar to others and therefore buy things that are bought by people whose tastes they want to share, even if they can only afford a fake copy. Retail strategies persuade people to express themselves in three stages: first when they buy it, second when they use it and third when they reuse it to fuel their own creativity.

Significantly, these changes were not mirrored elsewhere. Countries that were not part of the European Enlightenment and consequent industrialisation have not since overtaken those that were, with the dramatic exception of China. There are numerous interpretations of this divide. Jared Diamond emphasises biology and geography, while William Baumol and others prefer political and social structures. We are far from being able to deduce the reasons. But it is unarguable that, where Enlightenment principles did take root, creative economies later emerged, and where they did not, creative economies did not seem to come naturally.

Circles of Desire

The human desires behind this development were categorised by the American psychologist Abraham Maslow in his hierarchy of human needs. He suggested that our most basic needs, at the bottom, are our physical needs for air, water, food and sex. Only if these were satisfied, even temporarily, did we express needs for safety (security, stability) and then next for belonging, love and acceptance from family and friends. Next is the need for more generalised esteem from colleagues and even strangers. At the top is our need for self-actualisation or self-fulfilment.

Maslow spent years clarifying and refining what he meant by self-fulfilment, and in 1970, just before he died, he replaced the term with two others: the 'aesthetic' and the 'cognitive'. By 'aesthetic' he meant our appreciation of beauty, which is too often ignored in discussions of creativity. By 'cognitive' he meant our desire for knowledge and particularly for understanding knowledge (I refer to this later as 'creativity needs freedom'). As creativity is the most basic expression of self-fulfilment, it is tempting to put it at the top. I said in *The Creative Economy* that 'We should not be surprised if people, whose material needs are largely satisfied and who have a high level of disposable income, remix their ambitions and put a premium on matters of the mind'.[7] Any convincing notion of what is happening in the creative ecology has to take account of these psychological and aesthetic elements.

Searching for a Name

There have been many attempts to label these successive changes in people's relationship to ideas, information and knowledge. In the 1950s, building on Thorstein Veblen's ideas about 'conspicuous consumption', people began to talk about the *consumer society,* driven by advertising and exploiting rising incomes, as described in David Riesman's *The*

Lonely Crowd, William H. Whyte's *The Organisation Man* and Sloan Wilson's *The Man in the Gray Flannel Suit.* (I note in passing economist Joseph Schumpeter's remark a few years earlier that 'The evolution of the capitalist style of life could be easily - and perhaps most tellingly - described in terms of the genesis of the modern lounge suit'.)[8]

With the spread of computers, people talked of the *information society.* The ease with which computers generated data led to talk of information overload (some Asian societies are still worried about this). Meanwhile, Americans, enjoying the internet's sense of collaboration and community, talked of the *wired economy* and *network economy.* In Europe, realising that raw information was not enough, people preferred to speak of 'knowledge' and in 2004 the European Union adopted the *knowledge economy* as its slogan.

The Challenge: Bringing the Focus back to People

All these labels miss something vital. We need to recognise the dynamic process of individuals using ideas to explore and refashion their personal understanding of the world. We need to treat people not as economic units but as autonomous, thinking individuals. We also need to accept the fuzzy, contingent nature of knowledge.

The challenge is to integrate this new understanding of individual creativity with our wider understanding of social development. The theory of the creative ecology sets out a possible framework. It tries to answer these questions:

- What is the nature of creativity?
- What is the nature of creative work and the creative economy?

- What is their relation to other factors of change, such as innovation?
- How does a market in ideas operate?
- What should governments do, if anything?

At best, it provides a model of the way in which people actually have ideas and how they develop them, sometimes as work, sometimes not as work at all. It is a concept in evolution and appears in many guises, as is seen in the next chapter.

2

First Ideas

Counting Industries

Through the 1990s Britain's manufacturing industries were in steep decline. Faced with companies that were uncompetitive, badly managed and boring, many young people preferred to work in financial services and media, which were growing faster, were more fun and were better paid. Policy-makers were slow to recognise this shift. Prime Minister Tony Blair admitted in 1997 that Parliament might well debate declining jobs in the ship-building industry but would struggle to hold a debate on design.[1] Initially, his new government continued to push the old agenda. Its report that year on 'Competitiveness: A Benchmark for Business' mentioned printing but not publishing; its White Paper, 'Building the Knowledge-Driven Economy', mentioned knowledge not creativity; and its new childhood curriculum said that creativity applied only to the arts.[2]

So when the Department for Culture, Media and Sport (DCMS) wanted more money for the arts it had to convince the Treasury that it was business-like. It did so by redefining cultural activities as 'creative industries' and including some sectors not previously regarded as cultural (for example, advertising and software), and then collecting data to convince the Treasury that these industries employed more people and added more to the economy than had been assumed. Within a few years, minister Chris Smith's tireless campaigning meant that creative industries were seen as central to Britain's competitiveness. It is true that most creative people did not care much about global competitiveness and wanted to collaborate with anyone who was any good, wherever they happened to be, but everyone responded well to the ministerial enthusiasm.

The volte-face was dramatic. Twenty years earlier, Europe's radical sociologists and the Left had been hostile to Hollywood's success and attacked it for being a 'cultural industry', intending to be wholly derogatory. By 2000, the Labour government had reclassified film and other sectors as 'creative industries', intending to be wholly complimentary.

The British approach was based on thirteen industries: advertising, architecture, art and antiques, crafts, design, designer fashion, film and video, interactive leisure software, music, performing arts, publishing, software and computer services, and TV and radio. 'What?' one asks, 'No science, no research?' The original brief had included all activities that involve intellectual property, including patents, and so covered science and innovation, but pressures from other government departments persuaded the DCMS to stick to its own responsibilities for culture and to focus on copyright.

Since then, many other governments and analysts have used a variant of this basic model to categorise their own economy. The most notable work has been done in Europe, America, China, Australia, Brazil, Canada, Singapore and Hong Kong. My own 2001 list of fifteen industries added R&D and toys and games, and I referred to 'core' industries with significant multiplier effects, especially in media, advertising, design and software.

We should be careful. The word 'industry' is semantically misleading and statistically incomplete. It is true that it is used to refer to any group of like-minded companies, but it has never shaken off its roots in repetitive manufacturing and conjures up images of factories, smoke-stacks and unskilled workers (though considerable qualifications are needed to enter today's factories). It has become a metaphor for large-scale, repetitive mass production. To the extent that creative workers operate differently, which they do, the term is unwise.

It is also awkward to refer to people by a term they themselves would reject. Of the so-called 'creative industries' only a few actually refer to themselves as industries: music, publishing, TV, film, software, toys, video and perhaps crafts and fashion. There is a clear criterion: do we make something in multiple copies? If so, we are an industry. Businesses that are closer to the intangible (performing arts) or restrict themselves to unique objects (art) do not refer to themselves as industries. There is definitely an art market, one of the purest in the whole economy, but art is not an industry (except for the art factories in Dafen, China). Architects call themselves a profession and push the word out to the construction industry where people actually build things. Designers also think of themselves as a profession and only 40 per cent of British designers regard themselves as part of an industry. Craft is both a 'creative' industry and a 'manufacturing' industry.

It was ironic that the British and other governments adopted the term 'creative industry' at the precise moment that the internet was generating a whole universe of non-industrial ways of producing and distributing ideas. And, worse, that the policy-makers focused on those industries that were the most vulnerable to digital media and quickly found themselves in crisis.

For these reasons, we should welcome the trend away from lists of industries and towards activities. Although Britain's list attained almost iconic status, its 2008 'Creative Britain' report made scant reference to it and only as a means of organising data. Britain has moved on and now focuses on individuals and organisations trying to think for themselves and use their imaginations ('light bulb' moments), away from industry-centred institutions and towards people-centred processes.

Individuals and Occupations

It was known from the beginning that industries do not tell the whole story. It is true to say that a country's steel industry does contain all its steel companies and all its steel workers. But creative industries do not and never will contain all the people having new, interesting and commercially useful ideas. The nature of creative work means that industries are not the main characters in the story.

The large number of people who are full-time creative workers but work outside an industry requires an economic model based on individuals and what people do, or their occupation, rather than where people work in terms of structures and organisations. Richard Florida highlighted this occupational approach in *The Rise of the Creative Class* (2001) and many US state and city governments have picked up his ideas.

Over half (52 per cent) of Britons who say they are creative workers work outside a creative industry.[3] In America, the figure is about 50 per cent. In both countries, the proportion is higher in large cities than in small towns and rural areas. In London, 69 per cent of people with a creative occupation work in a creative industry, whereas in the rest of the country the proportion drops below 50 per cent. The exact numbers vary sector by sector.

In Australia, Queensland University of Technology has shown that 159,000 people with creative occupations work outside a creative industry, while 138,000 people work in creative occupations *in* creative industries, and an additional 147,000 work in management and support functions inside a creative industry.[4]

We need both models to get a rounded picture. Industry data gives us a bird's-eye view of the industry groupings that are the main drivers of TV, film and music and the main concern of government policy in these areas. However, these aggregated lumps of industry data conceal as much as they tell us. Florida's approach generates a more subtle and more multidimensional approach and helps us to relate creative work to the demographic and sociological conditions that facilitate it. It provides a useful antidote.

Cores and Circles

It is better still to move from the parts to the overall pattern, to encompass both the personal and the environment. So a third option is to focus on a centre of creative work surrounded by larger circles of intermediary and functional activities such as media and technology. My 2001 taxonomy spoke of the 'creative core'. Britain's BOP Consulting proposed a series of overlapping circles: (1) Creative Originals (for example, art), (2) Creative Content (music), (3) Creative Experiences (live performance), and (4) Creative Services (advertising).[5] The New England Foundation for the Arts, which represents six American states, prefers cultural core, cultural periphery and creative industries.[6]

The best-known of these models is the radiating circles produced by Kern European Affairs (KEA) in its report on 'The Economy of Culture in Europe', which was the first comprehensive analysis of the European situation.[7] KEA's four circles consist of (1) Cultural products that are non-industrial, (2) Cultural industries whose outputs are exclusively cultural, (3) Creative industries and activities that incorporate elements from the first two circles but whose outputs are functional, and (4) Related industries specialising in equipment to facilitate the use of copyright works.

KEA's model was picked up by the British Work Foundation in its report 'Staying Ahead' (2007) and given a commercial twist: (1) Core creative fields: commercial outputs with a 'high degree of expressive value' and copyright protection, (2) Cultural industries involving mass reproduction based on copyright (such as film), (3) Creative industries and activities (such as design), and (4) The rest of the economy.

The ambiguity of these descriptions, and the difficulty in separating each circle from its neighbour, illustrates the blurred relationship between the presumed endogenous core at the centre and the exogenous activities in the rest of the economy. It is difficult to decide what should be at the core, and what should be seen as less autonomous and creative and more dependent and functional. Continental Europeans tend to place art at the centre, the British prefer 'commercial outputs', and Americans and Asians favour innovation or technology. Some models conflate the spread of ideas in society with the business relationship between them. If a designer makes a breakthrough in typographic design (a 'light bulb' moment), does this happen at the core or in the outer circle of functionality?

Ways of Working

Lying at the heart of these models is the assumption that people who are creative think and work differently from others. We suspect this is true from the artists we meet and read about: they seem to have different values, different preoccupations and even different morals. They think and work differently. When we ourselves are creative, we get a glimpse of this. Artist Lucy Kimbell devised the Arts Council England phrase 'ways of working', which focuses on *what people actually think or do* rather than their formal occupation or their position in an industry. It has a different starting point.

Frank Barron spent much of his life studying psychology and creativity and managed to entice Norman Mailer and Truman Capote to California for several days of psychological tests. He said that when people were creative they were 'both more primitive and more cultivated, more destructive, a lot madder and a lot saner than the average person'. He reported that they had high ego-strength, a high endurance of disorder, and a predilection for complexity, which worked in concert with the ability to distil order from chaos. These highly creative people are different in degree, not in kind, from the rest of us. We are all a variety of the same species.

The focus on ways of working goes beyond people's formal occupation to their attitudes and behavioural patterns. It sees a virtue in being multidisciplinary and deals happily with artists, scientists, academics and anthropologists as well as people of no fixed career and no fixed abode as they determine to give fruit to their talents. It accepts that many people do not have a formal position in an organisation, let alone in an organisation that is part of an industry.

In the past, this view about creative thinkers having an oddball mentality has led business people to marginalise them. What happens when they become the main agent of change, even the symbol, of a new economy?

Relationships

Economists have puzzled over the treatment of knowledge and information as much as anyone. Their main trouble-spots have been classical economics' assumptions that individuals and organisations make *rational* decisions about the allocation *of scarce* resources in order to *maximise their wealth.*

The long-held assumption that people make rational decisions sits uncomfortably with our knowledge of how our brains actually work. We are sometimes rational and sometimes not; often, we believe we are being rational when an outside observer would say we are being irrational, either because the goal is not rational or because we are taking irrational steps to reach it. Second, many of the resources used in the creative process are not scarce, and even when they are (such as talent, energy and expertise) they do not become more or less scarce according to our purchasing decisions. The principle that economic systems tend to equilibrium is contradicted by evidence at the micro- and macro-level.

Even worse was economics' assumption that individuals seek to maximise their wealth and companies seek to maximise their profits. Common sense and everyday observation, increasingly underpinned by behavioural psychology, say that we seek multiple objectives of which maximising money is only one. Even when faced with two identical objects at different prices, not everyone always chooses the cheaper option. We often seek to maximise our own non-financial status and feelings and we often seek to assist other people over ourselves. Someone may look irrational in discounting a financial gain, when they have made a rational choice in favour of other objectives such as status or the opportunity to work with someone they will learn from. Economics cannot cope with an artist driven by his or her own passion, or a software programmer working on open-source software, or someone working for the fun of it.[8] Our pride in ownership (including our relationship to our own ideas) also may constrain us from maximising financial gain. These omissions might have been acceptable when the dominant economic model consisted of firms selling manufactured commodities to households but become absurd in a world based on individual creativity.

Overall, our new thinking in psychology and sociology, and our better understanding of creativity, means that the economic conundrum (infinite need, limited resources) collapses. Or, if not collapsed, it does seem severely tested.

Economics has made great strides to reinvent itself by borrowing ideas from other disciplines, especially behavioural psychology, sociology and risk analysis. Some of the most interesting work deals with the way in which humans handle knowledge. Economists John Nightingale and Jason Potts say:

> The autism of orthodoxy stems from its treatment of the human agent, who [it assumes] is mindless and does not interact with other agents. The broad solution is to develop a framework in which agents carry knowledge and interact with other agents to use and create knowledge.[9]

This reference to autism resonates with anyone who studied economics in the twentieth century, when the basic theories of supply and demand assumed 'perfect information', or that everyone knew everything.

Nightingale and Potts range far and wide for more reasonable theories, bringing together evolutionary economics, theories of self-organisation from systems theory and chaos theory, the cognitive dimensions of human behaviour and organisational ecology, and complex systems. They point out that these theories may be seen as unorthodox by economists but are in fact 'close relatives of very orthodox theories in other fields of science'. They treat creative industries not as 'an industry per se, but rather as an element of the innovation system of the whole economy' and see creative workers as specialists in conceptualising and enabling change.

Their thinking takes a dynamic approach in preference to the static optimisation approach of conventional market theories. Instead of assuming that supply and demand are fixed and can be resolved rationally around a price point, it assumes an interdependent evolution of preferences. These preferences may favour high prices as much as low ones. If a company's premium brand is based on high prices (for example, fashion) it will spend its profits on more marketing rather than lower prices.

The phrase 'evolutionary economics' echoes Joseph Schumpeter who said, 'The essential point to grasp is that in dealing with capitalism we are dealing with an evolutionary process'. In other words, economic growth depends upon adaptive efficiency. Whereas Schumpeter focused on the entrepreneur's skills in fomenting creative destruction, the creative ecology treats all individuals as potentially creative, thus generating greater scale and scope.

What's more, the flows of ideas and knowledge are not only from the core to the periphery but also inwards. In this model, the whole system 'uses' creativity as a resource and a means of growth. Rather than the core industries having multiple effects in the wider economy, as in the 'Cores and circles' model, the rest of the economy uses creativity to multiply itself.

It thus takes a holistic view of creativity and includes other factors of change such as education and learning. In these models, there is usually more than one equilibrium, if not an indefinitely large number. It regards the process of moving from one equilibrium to another as important as any equilibrium actually reached. Ecologists would agree.

The Map Is Not Reality

A Polish mathematician called Alfred Korzybski was fond of saying 'The map is not reality'.[10] Korzybski was born in Warsaw in 1879 when Germany and Russia had squeezed Poland off the map. But he was not only referring to his homeland's confused status. He was saying that we should not confuse reality with our descriptions of reality. He distrusted the tendency to use abstract qualities that in many cases were misleading or simply wrong. Rene Magritte played with the same idea when he inscribed his *Treachery of Images* picture of a pipe with the statement 'Ceci n'est pas une pipe'.

So, leaping forward, if I say that Matthew Carter, who designed the Verdana typeface found on every computer, is a wonderful designer, I could be right or I could be wrong. The only certainty is that he designed a wonderful typeface. Or if I refer to a new urban regeneration project such as Birmingham's Jewellery Quarter or Shanghai's Hi-Creative cluster, the only certainty is that the project has good buildings and facilities. It does not mean that creativity will blossom.

Korzybski's remark is a reality check. Each model of the creative economy is helpful but none captures the full four-dimensional reality of how people have ideas and make a business out of their ideas. The models based on industries help us to understand concentrated centres of large-scale work but do not capture what is happening elsewhere. The models based on occupations face a problem in defining a creative occupation. The models based on radiating circles face a problem about what to put in the centre: thinking? creativity? art? research? The models based on relationships downplay the reality of commercial negotiation. All the models face the problem about how to rank activities in terms of their balance of creativity and functionality. Some skate over the relationship between the individual and the group.

And there are other models passing unacknowledged like ships in the night. Day to day, the vast majority of creative activities take place informally wherever people happen to be. We are thinking, cultural and social beings before we are economic beings, and our creativity is not limited to commercial work. Universities and research centres have been arenas of debate for centuries, and their structures and processes have shaped the way we think, wrongly or rightly. For most creative people, cities provide a day-to-day context for what and how they think and how they behave. The internet provides another context for countless varieties of creativity on a massive scale. Are there any common elements?

Bigger than the Economy

We need a systems-based theory that takes account of all creative processes, including doing, performing and making, work done for free and for pay, and work done part-time and full-time. It has to encompass individuals, organisations (businesses, companies, public bodies), creative industries (the core industries) and cultural industries (creative industries that deal in culture). It has to include special cases such as creative clusters and creative cities and sub-groups like artists, scientists and the creative class.

It has to go far beyond the arts. The creative ecology is better described in social or even anthropological terms than as a specialist condition of the artist. It turns on how we try to make sense of and improve the world, which may result in art but which may lead to a new concept, a new machine, a new building or a new approach to urban transit. The physicist David Bohm said that real originality and creativity imply 'one does not work only in fields that are recognised in this way but that one is ready in each case to inquire for oneself as to whether there is or is not a fundamentally significant difference between the actual fact and one's preconceived notions that open up the possibility of creative and original work'. The results, he said, may be 'a scientific theory, a work of art, a building, a child who has been rightly brought up and educated'.[11]

The tendency today is to throw the net very wide. In 2007 the American National Conference on Creativity heard presentations from Vice-Admiral Robert Papp, the Chief of Staff of the US Coast Guard, and Deirdre Lee, Director of Management for the Federal Emergency Management Agency (FEMA). Later that year, the European Commission investigated the creative economy's impact on European agricultural policy, and in 2008 the Shanghai Academy of Social Sciences and Li Wuwei held a conference on 'creativity and agriculture', which discussed innovative ways of using the countryside. All these organisations saw creativity as a useful tool to invent better ways of doing something.

One can throw it too wide. Some scientists use 'creativity'

to describe all processes of change, from the atomic level to the cosmic level. Although I see what they mean, these processes lack any human agent or any sense of the purpose or self-awareness that seem to me to be necessary.

3

Scope and Scale

No Limits to Growth

In this chapter I suggest that the determining characteristics of creativity today are scope and scale. By scope, I mean the range of activities, from art installations to the branding of cheap manufactures. By scale, I mean the numbers and varieties of people involved.

The *scope* of today's creativity encompasses an extraordinary range of formats, goods and services, far beyond previously discrete clusters of arts, science or technology. Rolf Jensen, Joseph Pine, Michael Wolf and others have shown how we choose almost everything, from eggs to cars and banks, as well as arts, on the basis of our personal preference for their symbolic values; in other words, on what they mean to us.[1] The novelty premium of new meanings, whether offered by technology or by style, is the driver of new products and services throughout the entire economy.

We have become more self-aware of how we have ideas and how we use and reuse them. We take a self-conscious delight in our own creative processes. We are learning how the brain works and the interplay of consciousness, memory and expression. We are more confident of new ways of working and demand new attitudes to the ownership of ideas, as declared in the Adelphi Charter.[2]

We enjoy crossovers between art and science, between fashion and technology, between fact and fiction. Here are two stories of discovery. When Oscar Tusquet, the Catalan architect of the Alfredo Kraus auditorium in Gran Canaria, discovered that the Namibian fog-basking beetles obtain water in the desert by having special scalloped backs and leg-joints that collect dew, he scalloped the theatre's windows in the same shape to cool their surfaces. And Australian PTW Architects surrounded its National Aquatics Centre in Beijing (known as the Water Cube) with plastic shapes based on soap bubbles, whose curves are highly efficient at collecting heat which warms the pool inside.

The *scale* is also greater. The new economy involves not only a few outstanding individuals (though they exist) but millions of people on a large scale. In the rich countries, the core creative sectors contribute about 10 per cent of gross value added and indirectly involve about 50 per cent. In newly industrialising countries the core figure is not much less, though the indirect effects may be smaller.

It is speculative to calculate the exact ratio of core to context, whether by direct or indirect spillovers, since they range from sales attributed to designs and brands to the sales of equipment and accessories, but it is surely substantial and there are estimates of global multipliers of fivefold or more. A brand name can be dominant for decades. A drawing of a logo can become the chief factor in millions of consumers' decisions.

In the old-style repetitive economy, most people's work could only be done with other people's capital resources. Most people were employees dependent on land-owners, patrons, financial capital or large bureaucracies. In the creative economy, the physical capital required for production is distributed more widely and more equitably throughout society. Everyone has a brain. In the West, most people have access to computers and the internet. In the words of Ben Verwaayen, CEO of British Telecom, It takes a dog, a chair and a computer to be part of the global economic order. The dog to wake you up, the chair to sit down on and the computer to log-in to the world.'[3]

The management consultants McKinsey calculated that 45 per cent of British jobs require the workers to exercise their tacit knowledge, or talent, with America scoring 41 per cent and Germany 37 per cent on the same test.[4] China and India rated 25-26 per cent. Even more startling was the discovery that 70 per cent of new jobs in Britain and America require personal judgement. Murray Gell-Mann, who won the Nobel Prize for Physics in 1969, says the most important resource in the twenty-first century is a 'synthesising mind' which can decide what is important, rejecting everything else, follow it up and make sense of it and then communicate it to others.[5]

The news is not all good. McKinsey also discovered that companies whose employees exercise tacit judgement (such as banks and media companies) have more variable financial results than those that do not (freight companies, mining). The contrasts are greater online, where the dramatic economies of scale allow exponential increases in information or sales with trivial costs. The internet undercuts the traditional economics' view that services cannot be scaled.

The next section explores two characteristics of this scope and scale: their openness and responsiveness to individual actions, and their variety or diversity.

Everyone Can Have a Go

The creative ecology has very *low barriers to entry*. Writing, drawing, composing and other basic activities have no barriers at all, although education and spare time do help. More people want to be in the creative economy than current markets can sustain. American, British and French universities routinely produce more than enough graduates each year to supply many sectors' total needs. In the late 1990s, according to economist Richard Caves, American universities educated 14,000 classical music performers every year to fill annual orchestral vacancies of 350.[6] British universities educate twice as many media graduates as the industry can support commercially and as many architects.

This is a social disaster if these new graduates see their degrees as purely vocational. But it is surely acceptable if they regard them as part vocational and part general, and wholly reasonable if they use them to develop their minds and excel in a creative ecology. The frequent complaint that almost all artists, writers, musicians, craft-workers and performers do not make a living wage, while true, ignores this third possibility.

The assumption that everyone should be a full-time employee is old-fashioned, industrialist ideology. While some domains, especially the public services, need full-time, permanent staff, most domains thrive on more organic ways of working that are open to change and adaptation. Rather than bemoan excess supply, we should celebrate astonishing activity. We live in a creative ecology where everybody can have a go. No-one should not be taught to write on the grounds that they will never make a full-time living as a writer, and no-one should not be taught to make images because they will not get a full-time job as a film director. European elites used to learn Greek and Latin to develop their minds; their children learned about media to prepare for the media ecology. We now need to develop a well-worked-out curriculum for the creative ecologies where thinking is a proper job.

Although creativity has few barriers to entry except education and ambition, some creative businesses can face very high barriers of talent, capital, regulation and market power. The high proportion of individuals working on their own and the large numbers of micro, small and medium-sized businesses (94 per cent of British creative companies employ fewer than ten people) go hand-in-hand with a few large companies that dominate distribution, especially where they can achieve significant economies of scale.[7]

The height of the barriers to entry is a reliable indicator of where we are in the creative ecology. As we move towards global distribution gateways, the barriers go up. The music recording business is dominated by four companies (BMG, EMI, Warner Music and Sony) and the film industry by six Hollywood-based studios (Disney, Fox, Paramount, Sony,

Universal and Warner), and the only way to play has been through acquisition, as attempted by a range of outsiders, including Coca-Cola, Matsushita, Vivendi and Sony, with variable results. But the high profile of these corporations should not obscure the reality of how ideas come into being, nor the profound threats to traditional financing and distribution. Nor should their high profile let us forget that they are unusual. Creativity and innovation come more from small companies than from large ones.

Exponential Variety

This openness generates a wide variety of contradictory expressions, formats and products. I call this *exponential variety*. They are varied because they express personal meanings and they are contradictory because there is virtually no consensus. Creativity is not deferential. Its essence is to be new and different. The process is volatile and competitive.

There have been many statements of this kind of forceful variety. John Stuart Mill, in his masterwork *On Liberty* (1859), wanted 'full freedom to human nature to expand itself in innumerable and conflicting dimensions'. For him, as we become more self-fulfilled, we become more individualistic. Exponential variety (diversity, in ecological terms) fulfils an adaptive function. Art feeds off itself.

These two factors, *low barriers to entry* and *exponential variety,* result in a high level of volatility. Life in an ecology requires rapidly adaptive behaviour if an organism is to survive, let alone develop.

We should not be carried away by the opportunities on offer. Openness generates its own problems, because the large numbers of aspiring workers means competition is intense. The requirements for the two conditions to take part in the ecology (education and an ability to take risks, which often need hard cash) are not evenly spread around the population.

And while the West upholds individual expression as a fundamental right - or, to be more precise, upholds the individual's right to decide whether to be individual or to collaborate - Asian societies uphold social consensus. The Chinese believe that the good life depends on factors that are common to all and that as we become more developed so we become more united. Westerners tend towards the individual voice, but both views are changing, as we will see.

Autonomy and Openness

Looking at individual creativity according to these principles, we can see that it is marked by autonomy, an openness to new possibilities, and continuous learning. There is a sense of searching for an underlying new order and perhaps for beauty and harmony. Systemic characteristics include diversity and collaboration. Compared with previous emphases on institutions and mechanics, there are themes of fluidity and fuzziness, and of emergent thinking.

4

The Adaptive Mind

The Ecological Mindset

One science has made a particular concern of these themes of systemic diversity, communities and adaptation. The German biologist Ernst Haeckel was fond of new words, naming over 1,000 species, and he coined 'ecology' in 1866 to describe the study of how organisms relate to each other and to their outer world (the word 'environment' had not then been invented). Ecology seeks to answer the question 'Why here and not elsewhere?' Haeckel did not expect his baby to become a fully fledged science, but in this he was wrong. He died in 1919 after being the first to name the conflict just ended as the First World War, which he saw as an ecological disaster.

Haeckel's new word shares with 'economies' the Greek root of 'oikos', which means 'home', but it refers to *knowledge* about a living space rather than to *rules* for managing resources. It is the grown-up, expanded version of botany and natural history. The early naturalists focused their microscopes on birds and insects and loved to count them, put them in boxes and label them, priding themselves on displays of dead butterflies and stuffed birds. Ecologists stood back and tried to understand each organism in its *habitat,* where it lives, and to identify the special *niche* that it adapts to its use. Starting with flora and fauna in the wild (the wilder the better), they moved on to all animals and now all varieties of organisms in all environments, from savannahs to cities. They have widened the search from groups of the same species *(populations)* to groups of several different species *(communities)* and the relationships between communities and the environment (eco-systems). The Norwegian Arne Naess, who talked of an ecology of wisdom, also coined the phrase *deep ecology,* which puts nature at the heart of the eco-system. Overall, ecologists want to know why their subjects live where they do, and how. It is these general principles that are most relevant to us.

So ecologists study systems and relationships. Indeed, some writers use the words 'ecological' and 'systemic' interchangeably.[1] Ecology came of age at a time when many scientists were looking at systemic wholes rather than things-as-parts. Using these insights, which later became influential in Norbert Wiener's cybernetics and Claude Shannon's theories of network feedback, as well as in the development of the internet, ecologists sought to discover the systemic principles of animals in their habitats. In the 1940s, Raymond Lindemann and others showed how eco-systems revolve around a chain of consumption, based on energy flows.[2] Every eco-system has four basic elements: the inorganic (known as the abiotic environment), producers, consumers and decomposers. Foundation species (primary producers) harvest an energy source and turn it into biomass, which is consumed by other organisms (primary consumers), which are in turn consumed by others. The decomposers turn dead matter back into the foundation nutrients. So the bears that scratch the banks as they catch the salmon that swim up the Alaskan rivers to spawn also aerate the soil, so the dead fish carcasses feed nitrogen deep into the soil, which feeds the roots of the pine trees, which shelter the bears . . . and so it goes on.

If we are looking at systems, we need to be inclusive and holistic. When ecologists look at a river, they need to know about all the organisms (from larvae to fish to passing herons) that use it, as well as the factory upstream that is dumping rubbish. They need to know about biology, geography, meteorology and industrial manufacturing. Of all the natural sciences, ecology gives us the most tools to understand the current environmental crisis.

By including an awareness of the self and perception, deep ecology is especially relevant to creativity. Arne Naess used to say that the point of deep ecology is to ask deeper questions. Deep ecology has links with Taoism and Buddhism and explores the shared feelings of artists and scientists that they are each trying to make sense of the same world and trying to create or discover something new that, in physicist David Bohm's words, is 'whole and total, harmonious and beautiful'.[3]

I will discuss four aspects of ecological thinking that are relevant to creativity and innovation: diversity, change, learning and adaptation. I tread carefully in applying the life sciences to human behaviour and still more to human belief. Biological evolution, for example, is a testable and proven theory, whereas the evolution of ideas is a social construct that works best as a metaphor. I take heart from Richard Feynman's remark that most of modern science is metaphor, as well as from artists who believe that abstraction is reality.

Diversity

We know the excitement we feel when we see a new species or a new environment; new to us is good enough. We enjoy discovering and learning about our world, and being reassured that it is wonderfully variegated in spite of the known loss of many species each week. Variety is the spice of our life. The early botanists were profoundly moved by the diversity of species, genera and organisms, and Darwin regarded it as both nature's greatest achievement and nature's greatest resource.

This delight in diversity is not universal. Mice in a cornfield are not overjoyed when owls go hunting. They would be perplexed to discover that some humans regard owls as wise and subsidise their nesting boxes but dislike mice and trap them. Our own joy in species diversity is sometimes powered by our predatory nature. We would no doubt change our tune if bears began to multiply and eat us up.

We measure diversity by taking into account not only the number of species but the variety of their relationships with others above and below them in the energy chain. Ecologists see diversity as a powerful indicator of a range of possibilities rather than as a mark of any single species' individual success. It enhances the possibility of future variation and adaptation.

The effects can be seen in farming. A farm with mixed

crops is more robust than monoculture because the former maintains the soil's fertility. A mix of animals also benefits the farm by using fields at different seasons and feeding off manure at other times. Best of all is a combination of a rotated crop system and a mix of animals so the animals' feed and waste-products can fertilise the soil and the pasture's by-products such as hay and straw can provide fodder and bedding. Traditional farmers are experts at reusing seeds and recycling products. (One of the arguments against genetically modified seeds is that their patent-owners deliberately make them sterile so farmers cannot reuse them.) The more crops and animals, the greater the chance of survival if one harvest fails or the price falls. Mixed-use farms may lack the economies of scale of large-scale monoculture but are more flexible, more productive and more sustainable.[4]

Imagine a farm with mixed cereals and herds of different animals, each requiring different knowledge, attitudes and skills. The workforce will have multiple mental frameworks and ways of handling knowledge and be more robust than a workforce whose members all think alike. The workers will have more opportunities for learning. If one method fails, they can try others. It is not surprising that the word 'culture' was initially used in agriculture and horticulture. What makes us creative is our culture, both culture-as-anthropology, which includes beliefs, morals, manners, dress, food and so on, and culture-as-art or aesthetics.

We find a range of diverse cultures within our own species. At the broadest level, we categorise ourselves into races, nationalities, tribes and ethnic groups. For many years, race was the basic unit *(Billboard* magazine only changed its

'Race Music' category to 'Rhythm and Blues Music' as late as 1947). Nowadays, the 'ethnic group' is the more common phrase. The eminent biologist Julian Huxley popularised the use of ethnic groups over racial groups because he felt it was impossible to identify racial differences between populations. Huxley believed that cultural diversity plays the same role for the human species as does species variation for other species. Our cultural diversity opens our eyes every day to the fact of difference, and stimulates us to imagine possible and even impossible futures.

It manifests itself in the way we form patterns and concepts and how we use language. It affects the social boundaries between what we keep private and what we feel we can make public. It affects gender diversities and again the extent to which we feel able to display our gender choice.

Richard Florida uses a place's tolerance of gays as a prime indicator of its likelihood of supporting a creative class, partly because the proportion of gays and lesbians in a population seems an accurate measure of a creative economy and partly because it is relatively easy to quantify. A tolerant society welcomes (or at least tolerates) different histories, cultures, perspectives, beliefs, styles and languages, and accepts different ways of thinking and imagining.

Diversity, then, is the source of change and one of the chief regulators of how fast change happens.

Change

The dominant model of biological change is the theory of evolution proposed by Charles Darwin and Alfred Russel Wallace in the 1860s. This trumped the ideas espoused by

Jean-Baptiste Lamarck and others, including initially Darwin himself, that evolution proceeded by the inheritance of learned characteristics. Both Darwin and Wallace had independently observed nature's profligate variety, seeing that children born to the same parents have different characteristics. They also saw that more offspring were born than survived (the struggle for existence). Then came their big leap. They deduced that an organism that is more fit for a task is more likely to survive, measured by its greater capacity to reproduce and have descendants (the survival of the fittest). Over time, by being inherited, this non-random selection of random change would lead to new varieties and even new species.

Darwin and Wallace were unaware of their contemporary Gregor Mendel whose experiments with peas were demonstrating the existence of inherited traits. When Mendel's work was rediscovered decades later, genetics became a key part of evolution theory, even more so with Richard Dawkins' argument that the gene, not the organism, is the motor of evolution; that the gene (the replicator) uses the organism (the vehicle) rather than the other way around.

Without discounting the inherited genotype, there is still uncertainty about the extent to which the phenotype, consisting of an organism's physical characteristics, including those acquired culturally, has a role in evolution. The new systems biology gives more emphasis to the phenotype, saying that our minds have a greater degree of independence than strict Darwinism might imply and more than Dawkins allows. The American biologist Stephen Jay Gould took this line, and also suggested that evolution happens not in a continual development but in bursts of punctuated equilibrium. Another variant is the socio-biology or behavioural psychology developed by Edward O. Wilson, who suggested that evolution takes place at the population level and affects social position. For example, he believed that human generosity cannot be explained by Darwin's principle of the survival of the fittest.

Is there a gene for creativity? The answer is 'no' in the sense of a single gene causing a single characteristic that we would call creativity, because of the complexity of the process. However, there may well be genetic sequences that predispose people towards characteristics that assist creativity, such as reasoning, memory and spatial awareness. The study of epigenetics, which analyses the tags or markers that affect whether a gene is turned on or off, and that are inheritable without affecting the underlying DNA, also suggests that some switches might predispose for creative traits. There is little likelihood, however, of creative gene transplants or a creativity pill, because of the difficulty of isolating the creative process. There is much more research into genes for physical characteristics, since the genetic processes are simpler and the rewards more direct. The International Olympic Committee has been monitoring gene doping since 2001. But gene doping for creativity is primitive as yet. Other avenues are more promising.

Darwinian evolution gave us large brains relative to our bodies and a capacity for speech, probably both at about the same time, which are fundamental to our ability to think for ourselves and to create and invent. But it does not apply to *what* we think or, crucially, to what we pass on to our contemporaries or future generations. The process of transmission is different. Extrapolating the struggle for existence to a struggle for ideas is almost wilfully wrong, because it ignores the ways in which we share and collaborate. Whereas biological evolution proceeds by increasing divisions into separate species, cultural change occurs by borrowing and mixing; and whereas evolution is Mendelian (inherited, digital), cultural change is Lamarckian (learned, analogue).

We are not distinctive only because of our brains and other evolved physical attributes, most of which are more fully developed in other organisms. We are chiefly distinctive for our minds, our inner life. What we do best is culture: creating it and expressing it. And it is a fundamental principle of Darwinism that culture is learned and that learned characteristics do not affect our genes and cannot be genetically inherited. Richard Dawkins has a good analogy of the difference between inheritance and learning: 'The human engineer who first designed the jet engine simply threw the old propeller engine out and started afresh. Imagine the contraption he would have produced if he had been constrained to "evolve" his jet engine by changing a propeller engine one bit at a time, nut by nut, bolt by bolt!'[5]

One of the best examples of the difference is homo sapiens' optic nerve, which evolved over hundreds of thousands of years in the African savannah so they could spot predators before predators saw them. It hasn't changed much since then; in evolutionary terms we were in the savannah only yesterday. But our learned ability to create and understand visual images changes rapidly and within individual lives. Think of Cubism, which flourished over twenty years. The thrills and shocks of abstract art are partly caused by clashes between the evolved biological eye and an individual's learned perception. (This in no way diminishes its beauty or the artist's achievement.) It is the same with film. It is certain that as our eyes evolve we will lose the ability to be fooled by twenty-four frames a second of projected film, and, if so, cinema would die out; but the learned inventions of digital cinema and biometric displays will replace celluloid long before that happens.

But questions of purpose and intent are more problematic: hard to define and harder to discern. Darwinian change is progressive in the sense of generating better adaptive fitness to a particular way of life but undirectional in the sense of any greater purpose. A bacterium and an ape could be equally fit for their niche; and both could be evolving, in increasingly specialised ways, towards extinction. Dawkins says that the proposition 'that evolution represents progress towards man is a myth'. Metaphorically, art evolves whenever an artist puts a mark on a canvas; but the person who says that the results evince progress towards some known end is expressing a highly subjective view. Gould has a lovely analogy of St Marco in Venice, saying that an observer might believe that the arches had been shaped solely to support the spandrels where the artists put their mosaics.[6] In fact, the arches are what count, and the mosaics on the spandrels are infillers. Beautiful, yes, but optional.

Learning

How, then, do we exploit and change our ecological niche? I said in the introduction that the primary question is how we handle ideas, information and knowledge, both ours and other people's. How do we learn to do so?

Our ability to interpret what is out there and select one's

own adaptive behaviour is exhilarating and valuable. Again, compare it with genetic evolution. We cannot change our DNA, we can only inherit it. In contrast, learning is analogue. We can learn the parts we want, and we can learn them in our way and then we can change them. We can be elegant or we can muddle along. We can say 'Eureka!' or we can say 'Well, maybe, let's give it a try'. We can learn not only from our parents but from anyone. We can even learn from ourselves. It doesn't matter were we get ideas from; it only matters what we do with them.

Since we are generally in charge of what we learn and what we do with what we learn, there is no guarantee we will learn an exact copy of the original. In fact, the opposite is more common. We can misunderstand the original, innocently or wilfully; we can take bits out of context that interest us. We can get things right or plain wrong. But getting things wrong (incorrect) is not necessarily wrong (failure). The history of art and science is full of people doing something 'wrong' but, if they are alert, using the result to create something valuable. Louis Pasteur discovered immunisation after two tests had failed. After the first failure, he asked his assistant to carry out another test while he went on holiday; but the assistant didn't do as he was told. On his return, Pasteur was smart enough to realise that the two 'failures' revealed a new truth.

I want to clarify the difference between education, training and learning. *Education* is the government-led system for teaching children and young people up to college levels. Most countries have broadly similar education systems in terms of what is taught, and how, at least in the government's prescriptions if not in classroom practice, except for faith-based and totalitarian systems. All education systems teach some creativity, but after primary school most restrict it to art and story-telling. Few schools teach creativity as an integral element within the learning process; it would not play well with the majority of teachers or parents. *Training* teaches specific skills, usually vocational and ranging from language to life-skills and professional qualifications. Governments become involved in training because they want the population to be skilled and competitive, but most training courses are provided by private suppliers.

And then there is *learning*. Ask people how they discovered how to do what they are good at and, apart from full-time academics, almost everyone says they learned from experience, from friends and colleagues, from reading and talking and doing. They were not taught, they learned. Learning is personal, diverse and endless. It is self-motivated, self-managed and often self-financed. Education helps but only if it teaches us to learn. Learning is what we do in order to understand; education is what someone else does to us. Albert Camus said, 'An intellectual is someone whose mind watches itself.

The creative mind that does not learn from others or from itself will wither away just as certainly as an animal will die without food or an engine without fuel will stop. Tennessee Williams said, 'Security is a kind of death'. So is shutting off new knowledge. Stop learning and you die.

The British car manufacturers died in the 1970s because they believed they had nothing more to learn. Britain in the 1960s was famous for its funky youth culture, but this creative, radical Zeitgeist did not filter through to the British Leyland Motor Corporation (BLMC) and the other manufacturers in

Birmingham and Coventry who lost touch with their environment and began to implode. Six years after Ford launched its Cortina, BLMC still had not launched a new model to compete. Meanwhile, on the other side of the world, the Japanese, not hitherto famed for their creativity, were sensing the mood of British and American car buyers more successfully than did Birmingham or Detroit. Since then, Germany's VW, Mercedes and BMW, which are owned, designed and built in a country where manufacturing is still strong and attracts bright young graduates, continue to succeed while Britain's brands have been bought by Americans, Germans, Chinese and Indians. Shanghai Automotive Investment Corporation, China's biggest vehicle manufacturer, which has joint ventures with VW and General Motors and controls Rover and MG, is exploiting Shanghai's creative ecology by linking into the city's designers and stimulating smart local demand.

When learning, spread the net wide. When a British property company asked for my views on the next ten years (a typical corporate time-period bearing little relationship to the real world of either business or time), I asked their senior executives to write down their ideas. It was a thin list. So I asked them to ask everyone in the company. The list got better. Then I asked them to ask their suppliers, who came up with a marvellous list of ideas. Finally, I asked them to ask their competitors. The result was a fully rounded, comprehensive list, full of ideas that no-one on their own could have produced.

Learn to surprise yourself. In July 1889, when Vincent Van Gogh was painting masterpieces like *The Starry Night, Wheat Field, Field with Cypresses* and *Vincent's Bedroom,* he was reading Shakespeare's *Richard II, Henry IV* and *Henry V,* because, he wrote, 'these dramas were the least known to me'.[7]

The Indonesian diplomat Soedjatmoko had an acute phrase about the 'capacity to learn'. He believed that every social group has a particular hunger for learning which determines its development chances more so than any political, financial or technical factor. To maximise this capacity, he believed, 'people will have to cooperate together effectively at higher levels of individualisation'.[8]

Soedjatmoko was particularly impressed by the Nordic countries. The OECD's annual Programme for International Student Assessment (PISA), which measures fifty-six countries, usually awards top place to Finland, which has more people in higher education than any other country and the highest rate of per-capita innovation. The Finns' view is that their high scores are due not to professional excellence or classroom size (in other words, to Soedjatrnoko's technical factors) so much as their national character and ethnic makeup, expressed in their appetite for self-improvement - in other words, their wish to learn. Denmark has also pioneered holistic learning communities, such as the Kaospilot business course based on chaos theory, self-organising mechanisms and communities of practice.[9]

A group's learning capacity will increase as it has a wider variety of people to learn from. In the early twentieth century, British homes had daily deliveries of milk in open bottles. Several garden birds, notably robins and blue tits, began to perch on a bottle's rim and drink the rich cream at the top, leading to epigenetic changes in their digestive systems. Then, in the

1950s, the dairies put aluminium covers on the bottles. The blue tits learned how to pierce the foil, but the robins never did. The reason is that tits live in flocks but robins live alone.

We can learn from anyone, family, friends, colleagues, rivals or strangers - even teachers. Julia Middleton, the founder of the Common Purpose learning schemes, says: 'Don't get advice from people who think your idea is brilliant. Talk to the cynics. Then you know what you're up against.' She works by trial and error. In *The Crowd Within,* neuro-scientists Edward Vul and Harold Pashler show that people who were given two guesses at answering a question scored higher than those allowed only one.[10] They asked a group of people two questions and then asked half the group the same question immediately afterwards and the other half after three weeks. The average of the two answers compared with the first answer was 6.5 per cent more accurate for those who were asked again immediately and 16 per cent better for those asked after three weeks. As the authors say, 'a forced second guess contributes additional information'. The reason is a version of the 'wisdom of crowds'. Software writers like to say, 'More eyes, fewer bugs'. The mind learns by testing and revising. Learning by thinking.

One of the virtues of learning is that we can learn anywhere. The symbol of education is a school classroom with one teacher and rows of pupils at desks. The symbol of learning is the brain, because learning is an attitude of mind. We need to maximise the opportunities to exercise the brain by meeting, knowing and working with others. A creative ecology has a proliferation of systems, places, organisations and events to facilitate mutual interaction. It will have formal institutions, including places for education, training and research, as well as libraries and museums, and an abundance of informal places and spaces where people can meet and have conversations. It will have markets, cafes and clubs where people can come and go.

It will have a sympathetic society that allows us to learn from whomever we want and wherever we want without fear of censorship or disapproval. It will have a government that supports learning not just in its classrooms but in ordinary life. It will have intellectual property rules that allow those who wish to learn to do so without imbalanced prohibitions. Companies will not merely let managers make their own decisions within the framework of company policy but encourage all individuals, including those who are not managers, to contribute their knowledge. In the same way as individuals want to learn, so organisations want to become learning organisations. The best way to do this, whether in the R&D lab, office, studio or cafe, is conversation and dialogue.

Adaptation

We seldom have a neutral relationship with each other or with other species. Inside a habitat, each organism sets in motion a series of relations that will adapt both itself and the environment to improve the niche. An ecological niche is not the small sub-set of marketing jargon but any habitat where adaptation takes place to make it more suitable for an organism. One might say a habitat is 'out there', while a niche is the result of a systemic relationship between the habitat and the organism, usually in the organism's favour.

The varieties of relationships range from unconscious

imitation through to community sharing and more overt forms of collaboration and competition. They can be mapped along spectrums from conscious to unconscious and friendly to unfriendly. I will deal with four kinds: imitation, communities, collaboration and competition.

Imitation

Imitation is one of the easiest and quickest forms of adaptation. We continually *imitate* how to do things and, equally important, how not to do things, from family, colleagues, rivals and indeed anyone who has high status in our peer group. Our copying may be more like flattery than learning as normally understood. Children often imitate their parents without understanding the reason for their actions. Teachers use this copying instinct to instruct us in how to read and write and how to behave.

When we do understand the underlying purpose, imitation becomes a more powerful tool. If we watch an artist drawing an apple and simply imitate his actions without knowing what he is drawing or, indeed, understanding what drawing is, we will be reduced to waving an arm around and looking worried. If we realise that the artist is drawing something, we will begin to see sense in the movements. If we look at both the drawing and the apple, we will start to learn something, and then if we try to copy the process we will begin to be an artist. Imagine I am sitting alongside an artist and on my other side there is a series of twenty students in a row. If I try to copy the artist's drawing, and my neighbour copies my copy, and so on for nineteen more times, the twentieth drawing will hardly look like an apple at all. Similarly, if I try to draw the apple, and my neighbour copies my apple, and so on, the twentieth apple will be a splodge. But if we all try to copy the artist's process, checking our attempts against both the apple and the art, trying to make sense of the process, we will end up with something recognisably like an apple. We do best when we copy the process, not the product.[11]

While Richard Dawkins was writing *The Selfish Gene,* he was increasingly aware of another replicator using a vehicle to spread its messages. He says he first became aware of memes when he found himself unconsciously imitating a colleague. How, he wondered, did 'tunes, ideas, catchphrases, fashions, children's games, beliefs, and ways of making pots' spread around a community? He invented the word 'meme', from memetics, or imitation, to describe how ideas are transmitted around a population. Although evolution is commonly taken as a metaphor for social change, virology, epidemiology and the spread of infection may provide more relevant models.

The point about memes is that they are transmitted before anyone has coded or explained them. They are acquired, done, passed on and imitated again in a flash. Another important characteristic is that every incident is recognisably the same but always slightly different.

Biologist Susan Blackmore has proposed a technological meme, a 'teme', that spreads itself by means of information technology. She says the information transmitted in books, computers and the internet constitutes a new mix-and-match evolutionary process, and suggests we are on the verge of having 'teme machines that carry out all three processes of copying, varying and selecting information without us knowing'. This echoes Lawrence Lessig's belief that computer code has surreptitiously become a kind of 'private law'.[12] Black-more's theory of a third replicator lacks evidence but has strong metaphorical force.

Communities

We are more likely to imitate if we feel part of the same *community* as the person we are copying. We have seen how the blue tits were able to get to the milk, whereas the solitary robins went thirsty. The robins did not want to copy another species even when it was being manifestly successful in front of their eyes.

The presence of another organism of the same species makes it more attractive for subsequent organisms (known as mutualism or symbiosis). Larger populations can satisfy more of an individual's needs on a more regular basis. Ants, bees, wasps and termites are classed as the most extreme social animals, with the highest form of mutual aid; here, kinship operates more strongly between siblings than be-tween parents and children.

Look at the termites. When a few gather together they are literally useless and soon die. But when thousands gather they make wonderful nests with air-conditioning systems more efficient and ecologically sound than any human has yet achieved. This is not about scale on its own, because many larger groups of animals, humans included, correlate with greater violence. It is called mutualism, not collaboration, as each termite is scarcely aware of the choices it makes, if indeed they can be called choices. The termites do not col-laborate; they act unconsciously as one. They demonstrate perhaps the most common kind of relationship in the natural world, where organisms live mutually while unconscious of their shared bond. Grasses that benefit from frequent cropping thrive in meadows where animals frequently graze, but the grass and the animals cannot be said to be collaborating in any normal way. The girdling beetle which prunes the mimosa tree where she lays her eggs, thereby enabling the eggs to live, is unaware that she is extending the mimosa's life for itself as well as for other beetles like her. (Having finished the pruning, she falls to the ground and dies immediately.) When we seek to understand why humans enjoy symbiotic relationships with each other, are we able to say we can know them completely?

A smaller population of social organisms will have the opposite effect. Below a certain number it will die out. Ants and other extremely social animals cannot live alone. Health workers use this principle to control pests. Africans have reduced the numbers of the tsetse fly and thereby cut back on sleeping sickness, and the Chinese have virtually eliminated the water snails that were causing bilharzia in southern China. They did not have to eliminate all the snails; below a certain level the population failed to reproduce.

Our communities of mutual aid are based on domains or niches. Such communities have always existed, as Peter Kropotkin showed a hundred years ago in *Mutual Aid,* but the niches within a creative ecology reflect the more intimate, fluid and volatile nature of creative processes. They tend to be exclusive in that few individuals belong to more than one at the same time, though people can move between them over time. Each domain has its own aesthetic, language, structure and systems of reward and penalties, as well as its own style of clothes, manners and ethics. Danish sociologist Etienne Wenger has developed a similar idea of 'communities of practice' held together by shared meanings: 'As people pursue a shared enterprise they develop a common practice; that is, shared ways of doing things and relating to one another that allow them to achieve their joint purpose. Over time, the resulting practice becomes a recognisable bond.'[13]

If we look at the hinterland of notably creative people we often find a mixture of domain experiences. The inventor James Dyson trained as an artist, a designer and an engineer and uses all three communities in his work. He got the idea for his bagless cleaner when he saw an industrial saw cut through green wood without clogging its teeth. Five years and 5,127 prototypes later he produced his winning design. He is typical of the best manufacturers in mixing creativity, innovation, craft and engineering in a seamless circle. Japanese fashion designer Issey Miyake similarly combines a knowledge of fabrics, chemicals and colour with an acute sense of beauty to produce his clothes. In 2007 he asked Dyson to design the catwalk for his autumn show and then asked him to lend a hand with the clothes as well.

People like Dyson and Miyake treat everything as a potential source of inspiration; they treat everything as a playground. Or, to switch metaphors, they make full use of the commons described by biologist Garrett Hardin as organising communal resources for the public good. In contrast, the British car manufacturers exemplified the silo mentality of people who shrink their awareness of their surroundings and ignore what is happening around them. Many people live in a silo called arts or a silo called science, with little appreciation of each other (although matters have improved immensely since C. P. Snow said that Britain had 'two cultures').[14] Dyson and Miyake represent the other extreme of openness to and learning from each other's community in mutual symbiosis.

Both Apple and Microsoft are admired innovators but their innovation lies as much in systemic borrowing and cross-fertilisation as in-house research. Most of their core ideas and component software and hardware are originated by other companies and then licensed or bought. Many elements of the iPod were developed elsewhere, and Microsoft licensed what became Windows for $25,000, later upped to $75,000.

It does not matter where you get your ideas from; it only matters what you do with them.[15] In the case of the iPod, Apple changed not only its own computer domain but also the music domain. The music industry had been losing touch with artists and audiences for many years. The way was open for someone to generate a whole new domain based on enabling people to get the media content that they want, how they want, when they want and to pay as they want. Apple's change required adapting to a volatile niche.

Collaboration

The third relationship is collaboration, when two or more organisms or species deliberately cohabit and share for a specific, known benefit. This goes beyond mutualism and altruism in that the collaboration is learned and explicit and the participants are conscious of the deal. It may well grow out of a community, but it moves beyond community-based mutualism to more focused arrangements between two or more specific individuals. So someone in a community or domain as well as sharing experiences will use proximity to develop explicit collaborative processes. The increasing popularity of collaboration undercuts the paradigm of the Romantic Author and lone inventor (typically male) that dominated the arts and sciences throughout the eighteenth and nineteenth centuries. The new paradigm is the entrepreneur skilfully weaving recombinant creativity.

Once again, we can disentangle several different strands. In the arts, collaboration is often necessary for practical reasons. Most of the most popular cultural forms developed in the twentieth century, including film, radio, TV, magazines, pop and jazz, are unavoidably collaborative. Writing computer code and designing information networks and digital media are even more so. People born in the last twenty years are not only instinctively attuned to multimedia but are instinctively collaborative.

Another strand is the growing recognition of systems and emergent thinking. In systems thinking, no single part can articulate or represent the whole. Emergent thinking cannot be perceived from a single viewpoint but emerges from the whole. Openness to others, and to attempts to understand the whole, is a critical part of the process. Collaboration is more efficient, faster and likely to be more successful. It is more likely to attain the known objective and, perhaps even more importantly, to generate a stream of learning experiences that will throw up new ideas along the way.

As people strive for a new idea, they can be as competitive as anyone else, and, because creativity is novel and because we are putting our own ideas on the line every time, the competition can be personal and harsh. Yet it is tempered by endlessly looking over one's shoulder at what other people are doing. Charles Leadbeater sums up modern collaboration in his book *We-Think:*

> The basic argument is very simple. Most creativity is collaborative. It combines different views, disciplines and insights in new ways. The opportunities for creative collaboration are expanding the whole time. The number of people who could be participants in these creative conversations is going up largely thanks to the communications technologies that now give voice to many more people and make it easier for them to connect. As a result we are developing new ways to be innovative and creative at mass scale. We can be organised without having an organisation.[16]

Collaboration doesn't obviate individual talent or ignore the light bulb' moment. It doesn't ignore the moment when a musician or designer suddenly realises how to achieve the effect they want. But it does explain the way in which most people get to that point.

Newton famously said, 'If I have seen further, it is by standing on the shoulders of giants'. True to his principles, he borrowed this remark. Sociologist Robert Merton has traced it back at least to Bernard of Chartres, a twelfth-century theologian. The Indian poet Rabindranath Tagore was more robust: 'Oh Fool, to try to carry thyself upon thy own shoulders!'[17]

Competition

The fourth relationship is competition. In describing the battle for limited natural resources, Darwin's *On the Origin of Species* mentions competition, struggle, enemies, battle and even war.[18] These words reflected the thinking expressed ten years earlier by Lord Tennyson when he described nature as 'red in tooth and claw'. Darwin's words, inseparable from his main point about evolution, are often used today to explain and justify competition between people, companies and even countries as a win-lose conflict.

But ecology's understanding of competition is more subtle and more interesting than Darwin's words imply. Two organisms might compete for the same resource but the competition might be peaceful and might occur without the participants knowing they are competitors, which takes the edge off any real sense of conflict. For example, two animals may compete for a water supply in the sense that if one drinks then the other cannot, but the thirsty loser may be able to go elsewhere.

Competition in a creative ecology operates on two levels, the internal and the external. Internal competition arises because the person who is having an idea will strive to have the best possible idea. The competition is as much with oneself and one's interpretation of others as one strives to meet one's own internal standards of aesthetics and style. It is therefore common to find people collaborating at this stage in order to enable them to compete with their own notion of what might be possible.

When we launch our idea, it has to meet external requirements of novelty, meaning and utility and to fight for itself in the marketplace, and competition becomes much closer to normal business practice.

In market theory, competition is rightly seen as one of the main drivers of diversity and novelty as companies seek to differentiate themselves in the market. This is another reason why, as we will see in Chapter 9, creative freedom needs markets if it is to develop.

Let's Redesign the World

The popular use of 'eco' as meaning 'green' and 'environmentally friendly' is welcome if sometimes misleading. It can be misleading because the tsetse fly that devastates a savannah or the human who drives a 4 x 4 in a city centre is part of an ecology just as much as the tick-birds cleaning a rhino or a citizen who prefers to bicycle. But eco-literacy represents a welcome new sensitivity to the environment, or rather an old sensitivity that people in rich countries have not expressed for a long time. It springs from an awareness that humanity's ecology, which seemed to serve us so well, is dependent on our own ability to adapt.

Nobody would dispute that scientists know more about nature than ever before, as shown by developments in knowledge and technology. But there is a growing sense that the mainstream science shaped by Galileo, Bacon, Descartes and Newton is too reductionist and too much in love with facts and quantities. It has enabled the West to develop remarkable technology and innovation, and is now enabling other countries to do the same, but at the cost of relegating sensation and quality to the margins, to art. Art is now fighting back. Perhaps eco-creativity is the new Renaissance.

The swing back is coming not only from artists, designers and architects but also from quantum physics and biology. Fritjof Capra says that although physics initiated the new paradigm the dominant models are now biology and systems theory. He puts it well:

During the [20th century] the change from the mechanistic to the ecological paradigm has proceeded in different forms and at different speeds in various scientific fields. It is not a steady change. It involves scientific revolutions, backlashes and pendulum swings. A chaotic pendulum in the sense of chaos theory - oscillations that almost repeat themselves but not quite, seemingly random and yet forming a complex, highly organised pattern - would perhaps be the most appropriate contemporary metaphor. The basic tension is between the parts and the whole. The emphasis on the parts has been called mechanistic, reductionist or atomistic; the emphasis on the whole holistic, organismic or ecological.[19]

In my terms, it is the difference between being repetitive and being creative (as shown in the introduction, page 5).

In the same vein, the physicist David Heisenberg told his students to see the world as music, not as matter. Physicist David Bohm based his work on 'three interrelated factors: nature's unbroken and undivided movements; the inseparability of human experience from that movement; and the use of artistic and scientific sensibilities to discern the ever-changing meaning of what is fitting and the good within that movement'.[20]

During the Bali summit on global warming in 2007, there was a stand-off between the rich countries, who wanted all governments to set the same targets for reducing emissions, and the still-industrialising countries, who wanted lower targets to reflect their lower level of industrialisation. The poorer countries said that America was responsible for the bulk of the pollution and should bear the brunt of the reduction. One participant, Samdhong Rinpoche, a Buddhist monk, said, 'The challenge is to redesign the world: to design a more authentic, genuine and elegant world. Who needs this wasteful, stressful, congested, exploitative world where half humanity goes to bed hungry and the other half suffers from obesity? We can do better than this.'[21] We are back at the learning capacity of nations and the search for creative ecologies.

What did Bohm mean by saying we use science and arts to discern meaning? A creative ecology does not have to be sustainable in the sense of operating at a minimal level of energy or work. That is not the way. Rather, sustainability is using today's potential to the maximum without limiting future generations from doing the same. In a purely physical environment, minimalism may be a sensible strategy, given the second law of thermodynamics. In a creative ecology, where resources are infinite, it would be perverse.

What we need is a new balance between the integration of ideas and the self-assertion of the individual voice. On the one hand, a creative ecology will exhibit strong trends towards sharing, networking and collaboration; on the other, we need room for difference and disagreement.

5

Creative Places

Favourite Places

Where can we expect the ecology to nourish? Think of your favourite places where you feel free to explore ideas through learning and adapting and where change comes easiest. At the most basic level, you will be free of want and the other constraints identified by Maslow. You will feel free of fear, censorship and disapproval. You will be in a group or community where new ideas are welcome not only in formal 'let's-have-an-idea-now' sessions but at all times. There will be a sense that the purpose of the group is not to live off other people's ideas but to explore one's own ideas; to give, not just to receive. Instruction will be replaced by dialogue in which listening is as respected and enjoyable as speaking. Since it is impossible to anticipate a new idea or the appropriate group to develop it, you will have access to many different groups and the ability to form an indefinitely large number of new ones.

Look around and you will see many groups like this forming spontaneously and naturally. In this, they behave as do self-organising systems in chaos theory, being generated in response to changes in the outside environment, not internal demand, and extremely sensitive to the initial input although they can be deterministic thereafter. Some groups may need a nudge to get going, but they will also be sensitive to the circumstances of their birth, the first naming and defining. Ideas at this stage are tender creatures. Groups will be informal, collaborative and leaderless, but far from decision-less. Debate and argument will be brisk but within an environment of mutual benefit. Once the response is complete, the self-organising system dissolves.

This process can flourish in large organisations so long as they operate as a network of small groups. Small groups provide the healthiest humus. It is absolutely essential for the group to feel free to develop its life as it wishes in terms of membership, direction and style. Members have to trust each other, so all will enjoy transparency and empathy. It is possible to design buildings and spaces to encourage this flow of dialogue, but the energy of a dialogue can be tapped anywhere: in a room, outside, online.

Some of these self-organising dialogues may appear to be like brainstorming but they have different origins, purposes and forms. Brainstorming sessions have formal origins and operate with sharp boundaries of time and space. A creative dialogue is informal; it has no such boundaries; participants' energies flow at all times. The commencement moment may be sharply defined but its duration cannot be anticipated, its progress cannot be quantified and its ending may not even be noticed.

In a creative ecology one lives in this way because it is highly rewarding and highly productive. I said 'live' because people who are serious about working this way also live this way. To behave like this at work and to be rigid and negative at home is a recipe for confusion and despair. And just as people cannot be instructed to be creative, so they cannot be taught to listen and take part in a dialogue among equals. I was once asked for advice by a manager in a Chongqing company who said her bosses did not want her to be creative. The only possible advice was, change your job. The audience laughed because they knew the advice was right but also hard to follow.

There are many techniques for enabling a dialogue and stimulating creativity. My own RIDER system consists of Review, Incubation, Dreams, Excitement and Reality Checks, and I recommend jumping between the five experiences in any order. Edward de Bono's lateral thinking and Six Hats are rightly famous. Anja-Karina Pahl's ingenious PRIZM game combines the Russian TRIZ engineering method, biological studies of form, Buddhism, and concepts of flow and energy.

Buddhism pervades many current ideas about creativity. In contrast to Judaism, Christianity and Islam, known as the religions of the Book, Buddhism is more like a self-organising system. The Mahayana schools in India and China have a metaphor of Indra's Net which seems to picture the system of a creative ecology:

Far away in the heavenly abode of the great god Indra, there is a wonderful net which has been hung by some cunning artificer in such a manner that it stretches out infinitely in all directions. In accordance with the extravagant tastes of deities, the artificer has hung a single glittering jewel in each eye of the net, and since the net itself is infinite in dimension, the jewels are infinite in number. There hang the jewels, glittering like stars in the first magnitude, a wonderful sight to behold. If we now arbitrarily select one of these jewels for inspection and look closely at it, we will discover that in its polished surface there are reflected all the other jewels in the net, infinite in number. Not only that, but each of the jewels reflected in this one jewel is also reflecting all the other jewels, so that there is an infinite process occurring.[1]

Indra's Net has three characteristics: emptiness, inter-being and inter-penetration. Emptiness or formlessness indicates that reality has no permanent facts or qualities and that truth and meaning depend on the wisdom of the observer and on the flows of causation. It is not nihilism, believing firmly that stuff is out there but that its meaning and vitality depend on us. Second, everything is contingent, which is where Indra's Net comes closest to self-organising systems. Third, everything is contained in everything else. Each of the jewels in Indra's Net is reflected by and contained in every other jewel. This principle is called inter-penetration or inter-connectivity.

High-Energy Centres

Creativity can flourish anywhere and we can have a great idea sitting in the middle of a desert. But if we want to move beyond creativity to a creative ecology we require diversity, change, learning and adaptation with sufficiently large scope and scale. We need places with the most people, the most active markets, the appropriate built environment and the biggest broadband networks. There, learning is fastest, collaboration easiest and novelty most stimulating.

In the 1990s, three-quarters of European R&D was concentrated in ten urban areas.[2] In America in 2006, one-third of all patents came from companies based in the three states of California, New York and Texas. In Japan, Tokyo and Osaka dominate. It seems that everywhere there is a hierarchy of popularity. Within China, companies look first at the east coast hinterland and then the five major cities and, within each city, the favoured districts. At each step, governments and planning agencies offer enticements. If you don't need a factory or a warehouse, the choice is wider.

Cities have become icons of the creative economy: their startling new buildings, their crowds, clusters and cultural diversity, their elite stars and industry gatherings, their opportunities for dreaming, internships and starting work, their craziness, their high costs, and, out of all this, their exhilarating novelty and excellence.

Cyberspace has the crowds, clusters and diversity, the craziness, the opportunities for dreaming and working, and extraordinary novelty and excellence. It lacks the dramatic (and costly) buildings but more than compensates by having a conceptual architecture more fantastic than anything on the ground. Online users have reinvented a whole new vocabulary of networking, collaboration, user-generation and community.

Both niches offer stimulus in abundance. The topsoil that

nourishes all plants and animals consists of 45 per cent inert minerals, around one-quarter each of water and air and about 5 per cent of organic humus that converts the minerals into biomass and nutrients. A little humus goes a long way. The internet is almost pure humus, cities less so, but even the crowds, squalor and derelict buildings of today's cities add to the contrast and contribute to the stimulus.

Cities: Creative Magnets

Richard Florida has added a fourth T, 'Territorial Assets', to Talent, Tolerance and Technology as his criteria for the creative class. Charles Landry has popularised the 'creative city', saying, 'A creative milieu is a place, whether a cluster of buildings, a part of a city, a city as a whole, or a region, that contains the necessary pre-conditions in terms of hard and soft infrastructure to generate a flow of ideas and inventions'.[3] The London-based *Monocle* lifestyle magazine says bluntly that today every city wants to be a 'design capital, ecology champion, hub for knowledge and magnet for creatives'. Neville Mars, artistic director of the Beijing-based Dynamic City Foundation, talks of flash-urbanisation and cunning cities based entirely on market forces.

I first came across the idea of a 'creative city' in Cedric Price's 'ThinkBelt'. Cedric Price was a British architect who came to prominence with his proposal for a Fun Palace in London, saying:

Choose what you want to do or watch someone else doing it. Learn how to handle tools, paint, babies, machinery, or just listen to your favorite tune. Dance, talk or be lifted up to where you can see how other people make things work. Sit out over space with a drink and tune in to what's happening elsewhere in the city. Try starting a riot or beginning a painting; or just lie back and stare at the sky.[4]

His ThinkBelt' was a master-plan for The Potteries, five Staffordshire towns that had once dominated British pottery manufacture but had declined. It was a recipe for a 'city caused by learning' where, Price hoped, people could 'Think the Unthinkable'. His ideas never went beyond the drawing-board (but the ThinkBelt made a special impact on me because I was a student a few miles away at Keele, Britain's most experimental university). I also loved his plans for London's South Bank, which offered 'Doubt, Delight and Change'.

His dreams live on. Richard Florida says: 'Without diversity, without weirdness, without difference, without tolerance, a city will die. Cities don't need shopping malls and convention centres to be economically successful, they need eccentric and creative people.'[5] In introducing its favourite cities, *Monocle* says the most desirable qualities are good urban transport, green spaces, friendly people, nice cafes and 'a place you can take off your clothes and lie in the sun'.[6] It was in this spirit that the Fierce Arts collective installed sixteen pianos on the streets of Birmingham so passers-by could play them. No rules, no security; just the opportunity to play music at any time, day or night.

Cities have always been the most visible and most concentrated arenas for creativity and innovation. Peter Hall lists some of the archetypes: Athens in the fifth century BC, Florence in the fourteenth century, London between 1570 and 1620, Vienna in the late eighteenth century up to 1914, Paris in the 1890s, and Berlin between 1918 and 1933.[7] He is less enthusiastic about Los Angeles in the mid-twentieth century, which Reyner Banham described as an 'architecture of four ecologies': Surfurbia, Foothills, The Plains of Id and Autopia. But he recognised that people who lived in these cities were deeply conscious of being there, and proud of it too.

A global landmark was reached in 2007 when 50 per cent of the world's population were living in cities, and the United Nations predicted that 75 per cent will do so by 2050. Britain was the first country to pass the 50 per cent mark and did so 150 years ago in 1851, the year of the Great Exhibition. In 2007 over 90 per cent of Britons lived in cities, and almost 95 per cent of young people. In America in the same year 81 per cent of people lived in cities.

Cities score high on our four indicators of a creative ecology: diversity, change, learning and adaptation. One measure is the number of people who are foreign-born, because foreignness is a mark of diversity. In New York, 33 per cent are foreign-born, followed by London (27 per cent) and Paris (16 per cent).[8] Japan's restrictive immigration policy holds Tokyo's figure to 2 per cent. Shanghai does not release data for foreign-born residents, but the number of expatriates is reckoned to be 450,000 which is also about 2 per cent of the population. A university education is another useful indicator, because graduates tend to want to go on learning. In Paris, 31 per cent of the population has a BA (France guarantees a university place to everyone who passes the baccalaureate), followed by New York (30 per cent), London (28 per cent), Tokyo (23 per cent) and Shanghai (18 per cent).

This mix needs to be stirred to provoke change. A city's

larger scale and scope support a wide range of domains, each with its specialised expertise, research, financial resources, social networks, sophisticated labour markets and international connections, in turn supporting higher levels of supply and demand. The average will be high but the quality may be uneven, ranging from admirable excellence to many failures; however, this diversity is better for learning and collaboration than a collection of organisations all at the same level. Compared with repetitive, entropy-inducing industries that require a standardised workforce that turns up at the same time, goes home at the same time and gets a good night's sleep, the creative city flourishes with highly differentiated independently-minded people, including a number of oddballs who stay out late.

Only cities offer the organising facilities to translate thought into action on the spot, which is a good way to learn. Urban-based collaboration is one of the most powerful forces in contemporary social change. Jane Jacobs, who wrote the *The Death and Life of American Cities* in 1961, said later in *Cities and the Wealth of Nations* that 'the more fully niches are filled, the richer they are in means of supporting life . . . the more diversity the more flexibility because of what ecologists call homeostatic feedback loops meaning greater numbers of feedback for automatic self-correction'.[9]

Elizabeth Currid, author of *The Warhol Economy: How Fashion, Art and Music Drive New York City,* says city-wide clusters have three effects: creative people can mix with each other on business matters easily and spontaneously; they can participate in business-related social events; and they can live in the same neighbourhood and get to know each other's lifestyles (her example is buying milk in the morning next to the guy you want to work with).[10] According to Simon Evans, who runs Britain's annual Creative Clusters conferences, clusters encourage innovation and sharper competition and reassure investors and customers. They feel more alive.

Imagine walking in a city; in some places it's a pleasure, in others it's a bore. The most enjoyable cities have hundreds of public places and spaces with a multitude of diverse people and activities.

Free access is another touchstone of an open ecology so people can wander in and out at will. In the twentieth century, public libraries enabled people to read and learn without charge. Today, higher incomes and the internet have made public libraries less critical. What is required now is free access across a wide range of activities, including open-air events in squares, streets and parks. When Britain removed its museum charges in 2001, admissions jumped 2.7 million, 61 per cent, within a year.

Architect Jaime Lerner, the charismatic mayor of Curitiba in southern Brazil, invented the idea of 'Acupuntura urbana' to describe the insertion of buildings-as-events into the urban landscape to spice it up.[11] The godfather of urban acupuncture is Joern Utzon, who designed Sydney's Opera House, followed by Frank Gehry, whose Guggenheim Museum in Bilbao stimulated other Bilbaons to hire Zaha Hadid, Philippe Starck, Rafael Moneo and Cesar Pelli. (Architecture is a global language and most of the world's most iconic new buildings were designed by foreigners.) Many cities are decorated with wonderful coruscating buildings, such as Frank Gehry's Walt Disney Concert Hall in Los Angeles; Herzog & de Meuron's

Caixa Forum art museum in a converted 1899 power station in Madrid and their Birds-Nest Stadium in Beijing; Snøhetta's Opera House in Oslo; and Rem Koolhaas' CCTV Centre in Beijing. These buildings gladden the heart, although in contrast they emphasise the generally cheap and shoddy work being done day by day.

All cities are rightly proud of their newest and biggest, but the energy flows conducive to learning and adaptation need a variety of shapes and sizes. In 2007 a Chinese arts organiser invited a Danish group from the world's leading Children's Theatre Festival to a multi-city tour. The city governments wanted to show off their biggest venues, but the Danish director knew that his actors work best with small audiences where they can make eye-contact with the children. One wanted intimacy, the other wanted to make a big splash. Cities need nooks and crannies, small, informal, private places to experiment. London's fringe theatre would not have emerged in the 1970s unless pub owners had been willing to rent out unused back-rooms to attract new customers.

In ecological terms, cities are prime energy exchangers. They attract people who are both producers and buyers: people who want to learn, adapt and explore new perceptions and who are discriminating and spend above-average amounts on novelty and style (smart demand). The two forces spark off each other. In the creative ecology, demand has an increasing marginal utility (in other words, an increase in demand leads to a further and higher increase in supply) and so generates more numerous and smarter outputs. Only a creative city can sustain the high level of smart demand that creative individuals need.

The focus now is on sustainability. Can cities, for so long the most wasteful of environments, take the lead in creating sustainable eco-systems? The two-week-long City Eco-Lab in St Etienne, France, in 2008 brought together hundreds of artists, scientists, designers and innovators to show how this might be done. Their projects included a map of local food sources; a green waste service; the use of hundreds of bicycles for food deliveries as well as for people; a city-wide car-share scheme; social enterprises; scenarios for 'eco quarters'; ideas for re-energising Le Furan, the city's built-over river, alongside reports from Melbourne and Rotterdam about their innovative plans to become water cities; plans for a community-wide energy dashboard; and above all a tool-kit for people to start their own initiatives. St Etienne's Eco-Lab was one of many similar events in which people used their creative skills, expressed in artistic, design, architecture and engineering terms, or just in terms of trying out something new. And did so according to the principles of diversity, imitation, community and collaboration developed so vividly by the internet.

The Internet: The World's Most Adaptive Market

If writing, composing and making videos, writing computer code, and the editorial skills of graphics and typography are creative skills, which they definitely are, then the internet has sparked the greatest burst of creativity the world has ever seen. Most of this is made by what used to be called the public or the consumer.

Until March 1989 the internet was a point-to-point network like the telephone and anyone who wanted to send a message had to provide an address for each recipient. They couldn't say, 'This is for everyone'. Like other users, Englishman Tim Berners-Lee, working in Geneva, was frustrated when he wanted to circulate a message to new arrivals or people who were in the building temporarily because he didn't have their address. His proposal, complete with what he called 'dotty diagrams', invented a space to which he could post stuff (hypertext) and everyone could read it and share it.[12] He played with naming it the 'Mine of Information' (moi), possibly an ironic reference to Miss Piggy in TV's *The Muppets* or 'the information mine' (tim) but plumped for World Wide Web.

Although Berners-Lee invented the Web to solve the problem of getting stuff to a few dozen people, the result is a sprawling marketplace with vast scope and scale as well as easy access and exponential variety. Berners-Lee is a typical example of how the internet develops. He is part of an unpaid community that from the beginning had minimal rules on ownership, control or operation and was committed to openness and collaboration. It is the biggest self-help, self-organising experiment in history and has produced not only Wikipedia, YouTube and blogs but countless flash groups formed around a specific issue and often lasting only a few days. It shows that, unlike the assumptions still held in most corporate businesses and governments, people do not always need bosses or clear lines of responsibility in order to be creative, innovative and productive.

Imagine if Berners-Lee had asked his research bosses for permission. Or if Larry Page and Sergey Brin, then graduate students at Stanford, had asked the university for permission to start a search engine. The dean would have required them to consult with the librarian who would have corrected the spelling of googol and the idea would have sunk. Or if Jeff Bezos had asked Barnes & Noble for advice on setting up Amazon.

Like thousands of other people, these pioneers are developing an alternative to the industrial, repetitive means of production and distribution that have dominated news, information, knowledge and mass entertainment for over a hundred years and, as a result of their technology and capital-intensive structures, have led publishing, cinema, recorded music, radio and television to become concentrated, homogenous industries. The internet has different roots: it is cheap, informal, fragmented, decentralised and alternative. The Yale professor Yochai Benkler says that its alternative nature stems from its 'institutional ecology' consisting of three layers: the physical wired networks; the logic-based standards, protocols and software; and the content.[13]

It proceeds by collaboration and markets-as-gossip rather than by contracts and markets-as-price. By removing the physical constraints on production and by providing free distribution, the internet puts the means of production into the user's hands. Conventional economics is centred on companies using people. In contrast, the internet, like the rest of the creative ecology, is centred on individuals using companies. Its growth is a major reason why the scale and scope of today's creative economy is so vast.

The internet may mark the end of the thesis put forward by John Stuart Mill and formulated in modern terms by Ronald Coase that the firm is the most efficient way of organising people and resources. I say 'may', because it is not certain yet whether the internet will continue to fragment formal institutions, as now, or generate new ones.

The internet's greatest impact is on individual autonomy and network collaboration. These may seem mutually incompatible. How can one process, one medium, increase both autonomy and collaboration? But that is exactly what the internet does.

Autonomy comes from exercising choices. It has always been true that most ideas are produced by individuals for their own personal, local enjoyment. The most popular form of user-generated innovation is a conversation between two friends; and no-one copyrights conversation. On the internet, these conversations, with full-colour video, can be digitally formatted and distributed (or should that be published?), immediately and freely, to one person or a billion. The Web has generated a growth in media markets and what Americans call 'social markets'. The ClueTrain Manifesto, published online, described 'markets as conversations' and says markets in media content are 'conversations about conversations'.[14] When these 'conversations about conversations' were restricted to small groups of people, few could participate. Today, they can include most of the population.

The other side of the coin is collaboration. The size of the one-to-many networks built by the old media corporations like a radio or TV network could be calculated by the number of receivers; a network with twenty members has a value of twenty. The value of a many-to-many network like a telephone network or an email network, as Robert Metcalfe showed, is twenty times twenty, or 400. The value of a network whose members are also members of other networks is exponentially larger. David Reed, who realised what he called the law of the pack in 2001, says it is two to the power of twenty (less twenty, less one, to be precise).

These hacking, blogging networks are not like road and rail networks or even telephone networks. Internet users began to talk about 'communities' but that is too limiting. A better word is eco-system, as in the micro-blogging eco-systems of Twitter and FriendFeed, where different communities live in more or less amity, feeding off each other, recycling energy endlessly.

The Danish toy company Lego discovered this in 1997 within a few weeks of launching its MindStorms robot system, when over a thousand hackers opened the operating system, improved it and posted their work online. Lego's instinct was to fight back, but wisely it decided to accept the improvements and now posts them on its own website. Eric von Hippel of MIT, who invented the terms 'lead users' and 'user innovation', shows how BMW actively solicits drivers who are interested in improving its cars.[15] General Electric's healthcare division works closely with doctors and medical researchers. Asia's Massive Multi-Player On-line Games (MMOG) companies have grown on the back of a continual stream of ideas from their most active players. They allow free basic access but charge players for special avatars and higher levels, with the enticement that such players get the chance to contribute new ideas. America's Electronic Arts moved in the same direction in 2008. Many companies post problems on InnoCentive.com, which offers large cash rewards to people who can solve problems. Anyone can post a problem or submit a solution.

Don Tapscott's Wikinomics reinvents the firm as a network.[16] He says that the trend to ask unpaid users and amateurs to contribute is inefficient; it is much better to ask experts who are not involved to be involved and to pay them *(the network office)*. Honda and other Japanese car manufacturers grew by operating as central assembly units for thousands of small family firms. Chinese motorcycle manufacturers in Chongqing are forming themselves into multiple informal networks along Japanese lines. These are not Californian hackers but low-paid Sichuanese factory workers who think this is the best way to go.

The evolution of NASA sums up the change. In the 1960s, NASA symbolised the best of state-run innovation. Today, it finds that amateur Click-Workers can analyse its data as well as can trained experts. Its *Phoenix* lander used Twitter to release the first news of water on Mars: 1 can now say I am the first mission on Mars to touch and taste the water'. (Twitter also got news of China's 2008 earthquake before any professional news agency.) The search for extra-terrestrial intelligence, seti@home, uses personal computers' downtime to provide the world's most powerful super-computer. Unlike natural eco-systems, where entropy leads to diminishing returns, ideas and knowledge go on forever.

6

Negotiating Uncertainity

Doing by Thinking

Being creative can be lonely. The British think-tank Demos joked in its report on creative industries, *So, What Do You Actually Do?*[1] Charles Leadbeater had given his answer earlier: *Living on Thin Air.*[2] It is hard to discern what Leadbeater and others like him do, although he is clearly very good at it. He thinks, listens, has ideas, talks to people and writes books. These are ancient roles, feeding off diversity and change and using learning to encourage adaptation, but are now seen as central to the way we live and, more importantly, work.

If we want to turn an idea into money, we have to negotiate a contract. What an idea is, what it means, who controls it and who makes money depends on words on paper. Whereas in the physical economy possession is said to be nine points of the law, in the creative ecology a contract is worth ten points. I suspect there are more contracts in the creative ecology than outside because of the large number of independent workers and the novelty principle, although there is no data, as far as I am aware. There are certainly more lawyers.

This chapter looks at how people behave when they develop and negotiate ideas. Of all the chapters, it gets closest to conventional microeconomics, because it deals with the interaction of supply and demand. It describes what happens when two or more people negotiate their relative influence over the future of an idea. Creative workers need to be expert in knowing when to move to a formal agreement. Too soon can be as problematic as too late.

Throughout, it refers to creative people and creative workers and sometimes just to people. The former may be more descriptive but the latter seems more elegant.

The Ten Factors

The main factors in these negotiations are:

- Serial change
- Niches
- The personal difference
- Novelty
- Meaning is uncertain
- Value is uncertain
- Demand is uncertain
- The network office
- Copyright is currency
- Mixed portfolios.

Serial Change

Every idea starts with a 'light bulb' moment and goes through a succession of changes and adaptations during which many people contribute to defining and naming it and estimating its potential worth. The process is endless: it starts with one person (or a few), continues with everyone who participates in developing and producing it and lives on in the minds of everyone who experiences it, even after the author's death. Each contribution is a stepping-stone to the next. As a result, ideas never settle but continue to reverberate in the mind: in the mind of the original thinker, in the minds of co-workers and in the minds of observers.

This process is reflected in the serial nature of contracts. Some of these will be between people with different assets; say, between a novelist and a publisher, or an inventor and an investor, or a producer and a technical team with multiple skills. American economist Richard Caves, who pioneered the analysis of creative workers' contracts, showed that most contracts involve people with very different skills: what he called 'a motley crew'.

Serial change is different. It occurs because turning an idea into a product involves a series of contracts, some of which will be between people with the same skill and some between people with different skills. As collaboration becomes the norm, so more kinds of creative development will require a lengthy series of negotiations between people with the same or adjacent skills.

In this process, a seller will want to sell to someone whose resources of finance, expertise, reputation and so on will enhance the work's latent value and increase the rewards proportionately, but the seller also faces the risk that the buyer will take it in a different direction altogether. There are parallels in corporate restructuring and refinancing, where early investors can be diluted to the point where they lose voting and economic rights. A skilful negotiator can ensure that subsequent contracts do not diminish their original economic rights, although editorial control is another matter.

Each transaction depends on how much the seller wants to gain future resources and how much a buyer wants the seller's asset at that moment. The seller and the buyer have to calculate their fixed costs and marginal income and thus quantify their own risk-reward profiles and try to estimate each other's profile. Each contract will specify the opportunities for subsequent contracts to change this risk-reward balance. The seller and the buyer can then estimate whether the risks are worth the rewards. At worst, they try to recover their share of marginal cost. At best, they will maintain their own value, gain extra resources and enhance the likelihood of future income.

Understanding the serial nature of ideas helps to understand how value arises. The theory of the value chain was developed by Harvard professor Michael Porter in the 1980s to explain how companies can be more competitive by adding value at each stage of production. The added value is not the excess of price over cost but any increase in value that affects the product's ability to move on to the next stage of the chain. Ideally, the total should be more than the sum of the individual parts. For example, a bad idea and a good idea (such as a script or prototype) may cost the same, but only a good idea will be able to move further along the value chain. In practice, sellers want to increase the perceived value of their assets so buyers will contribute extra resources.

Niches

A niche is the domain in the eco-system in which an idea is born and will live or die. It is impossible to be creative in the abstract and every idea comes out of its own niche and, in a sense, goes back into it. Each new idea has to fight for recognition in its own niche and an idea that is useful in one niche will be meaningless and useless in another and possibly not even novel.

It is a place you feel comfortable in: you know the people who live there and what they are up to. If you can't find the right domain or niche, invent one. We succeed more quickly if we know all about our niche and where the gaps are, working as a photographer selects a shot, by looking for new angles, sharp contrasts, curious overlaps and little-known gaps.

Each niche has its own ways of working, characterised by its inputs and outputs, its dependence on formal training, ethics, social status, the balance of individual work and group work, technology, regulation (how dependent is it on public regulation?), risk-reward profiles and capital requirements (how much do you need and where will it come from?), industry structure (freelancers or big companies?), personal lifestyle, working on one's own or in a company (personal people-led or network-led), financial rewards (how much, when, how equitable?), aesthetics (visual or verbal), intellectual property (important? copyright or patents?) and average take-home pay levels. Each niche's mix of attributes attracts some people and repels others.

To outsiders, a niche often appears similar to an industry (for example, bio-tech, financial services, TV), but these categories are too crude for insiders who prefer to use more precise terms. Film writers, actors and directors never say that they work in the film business when talking among themselves; they refer to the much smaller niches they are actually inhabiting, saying, 'I am writing this . . .' or 1 am playing this . . .' or 'I am doing this . . .'

The one general principle, therefore, is to choose the right niche, to know it intimately and to work within it.

The Personal Difference

As people join the ecology, and start to experience change, learning and adaptation, they will express their diverse idiosyncrasies and personal priorities both in their own work and in how they respond to other people's work. This *personal difference* means that creative workers feel personally committed to their work. They become passionately involved in the process and the outcome; they talk about 'giving birth to' an idea; they say they love it. This is why plagiarising another person's work is regarded as morally more odious than infringing copyright.

It also leads people to define themselves by their work, which in turn brings identity, status, reputation and even fame. Office employees borrow identity and status from their employer, but creative workers, unless attached to an organisation or company (as we have seen, a minority), have to build their own. This can be difficult and takes time, with luck playing a role, but, once gained, identity and reputation are mobile and transferable.

Working this way often involves putting personal considerations above commercial ones; for example, putting personal beliefs about beauty, or about a personal relationship, above considerations of financial gain (what Richard Caves calls 'art for art's sake'). This can be arrogance but it can be a sensible long-term strategy. Someone may reasonably decide to trade off economic rewards to obtain personal rewards, present or future, which they judge to be worth more. For example, they may decide to work with a well-known, high-status person for less than they normally change. Such a strategy may look like an indulgence but may be rational and commercial. Creative workers are just as prone to be irrational as anyone else, but their risk-reward profile is different.

Novelty

We have seen that a hallmark of the creative process is continual change and adaptation. A plant adapts by becoming better at exploiting its position in a niche, usually measured by its place in the energy chain. Creative people adapt to their niche by wanting to enhance it (see the 'dreaming' questions in Chapter 9). Their view of enhancement may not be shared by anyone else, then or later. It is enough that they think they are making a change.

Novelty can mean novel to a person, novel to a person in a specific circumstance or historically unique. Some outputs achieve value by being unique and staying so; for example, art dealers protect uniqueness by restricting supply to drive up prices (*artists don't advertise*). In contrast, other outputs accrue more value to the extent that they can be copied; for example, publishers want to produce as many copies as possible and to protect the copies.

Attitudes to novelty vary widely between different sectors. At one extreme, someone can write a line of computer code or upload an image to YouTube without knowing or caring whether anyone else has already done the same, and the discovery that the work was a repeat or was itself later copied would be likely to provoke a wry smile and a sense of community as much as indignation. On the other hand, a pharmaceutical company or a broadcaster that is considering a major investment needs to make its outputs really exclusive or unique. Intellectual property laws reflect these different meanings. Copyright law requires novelty in a specific circumstance, and so two people writing the same words may both claim copyright. In other words, the law makes no presumption of copying. In contrast, patent law requires the applicant to demonstrate uniqueness. If uniqueness cannot be proved, copying is presumed.

Attitudes to novelty also vary between cultures. People in Europe and America put a pre-eminent value on individual expression and novelty, while Asia and the Middle East privilege the place of an artist and the work within a tradition. This cultural difference carries over to contract negotiations, which tend to be more respectful of the individual creative person in the West than they are elsewhere.

Meaning Is Uncertain

Creativity has value because it expresses *meaning*. Sometimes the meaning will be obvious and widely accepted; and sometimes it will be hidden or contentious; and as an idea goes through the serial process of change and adaptation, so its meaning may change. Claims about what something means are usually more important than what it is.

The testable facts of science might seem to offer a certainty lacking in the arts, in that the former can be proved by experiment whereas the latter are subjective. In practice, the facts and natural laws that are most incontestable are held in common by all people and cannot be made private. (Patent law specifically excludes mathematical theories and rules, as well as anything that does not have a technical effect, though patent lawyers disagree strongly about the patentability of computer code.) Moreover, the difference in terms of potential future value is arguable in both cases. Differences of opinions over what an idea might be worth can be as vigorous in science and technology as in art, with each side trying to maximise its own stake and to achieve the greatest access to future resources.

The person who has an idea generally claims to know its meaning better than anyone else does, although they may not communicate the meaning to others, either because of a desire for confidentiality or a literal inability to put something new into words. Anyway, others may privately disagree with what they are told and suggest their own meanings to leverage their negotiating position. Everyone who joins the value chain gains an opportunity to put forward their own interpretation of meaning.

Artists add their own twist to this uncertainty. Some contemporary artists and musicians claim that while their work may be art it has no meaning; it simply is. This ups the uncertainty to new levels. Many artists play around with this ambiguity. There is no right or wrong, only a series of successive views about what something means (the *serial* factor).

Value Is Uncertain

Because meanings are volatile, it is difficult to estimate their value. It is hard to value inputs that are based on people's histories, experiences, skills and a range of largely unknowable associations and borrowings. It is hard to value outputs because they are novel. If you ask someone to have an idea for a script, a plan, a style, today it will be different from the idea they had yesterday; at least, both you and they hope it will be. In many cases, the values only become fixed insofar as the inputs or outputs have a contractual valuation.

It is sometimes tempting to set meanings early in the process, but it can be unhelpful: unhelpful creatively because it closes off future options and unhelpful commercially because it prevents future increases (although, of course, it also protects against loss). People thinking abstractedly about a story or a style want to keep their options open as long as possible, even if they have a private notion of its take-up, and it is hardly unknown for people to change their minds about what they are doing. As already stated, their views about value are likely to change as more people buy the rights to make their own contribution. Both seller and buyer are free to play around with the idea so long as neither breaks the contract, whether by changing the basic concept or by extending their rights over it in time (say, into future years) or space (say, into a new niche).

Previous contributors may benefit or lose. This can occur

vertically between people or horizontally over time. A worker is continually faced with a choice: whether to use ideas to produce more ideas or to focus on one idea and embed it in a product. The decision involves complex factors, such as the calculation of novelty and value and the ability to claim intellectual property as well as access to the resources required to be successful, and who owns those resources.

Demand Is Uncertain

It follows from these principles that, when people buy products to express their own personalities, it is also difficult to estimate *demand.* Sales figures for previous products are of little help, since the new one is, by definition, novel.

It would be absurd to try to quantify the demand for creativity, for new ideas. The more the merrier, surely. Even with creative products there is no easy answer. There is a known level of demand for going to the cinema and buying clothes, as shown by suppliers' revenues staying within a small range year after year, but each film or design is unique or at least novel and has no historic sales pattern or guaranteed market niche. Screenwriter William Goldman summed this up in his *nobody knows anything* aphorism.

We can analyse the history of past products, but this seldom reveals why some succeed and others fail. A creative worker may be more satisfied than usual with his or her output, but that does not directly translate into marketplace approval. As a result, it is almost impossible to accumulate useful sales experience. People who are experienced in their own domain and even those who have a record of success still make mistakes. (Dick Rowe, the Decca manager who signed the Rolling Stones to their first recording label, had previously turned down the Beatles, and J.K. Rowling's first Harry Potter novel was rejected by at least twelve publishers.)

A higher cost ensures neither proportionally higher revenues, let alone profit, nor more certain revenues. A buyer's perception of value or meaning is seldom related to the product's cost, although the amount spent on advertising can correlate with demand, as seen in both manufactured goods (say, fashion) and media (say, films). Price may be a better guide, because it will reflect demand at most points of the demand curve, but many prices are constrained by distribution and retail factors, such as the desire to recover the seller's sunk costs and to minimise the sales staff's flexibility. Sellers of airline tickets can play with a variety of price discrimination software tools, and theatres have followed suit, but the economics of cinemas and music venues mean that their prices are fairly inflexible. Music promoters can set the ticket price to reflect an act's previous sales, but cannot adjust it in the light of subsequent demand. Cinemas, under pressure from distributors, charge the same for a $100 million film as for one costing one-tenth as much.

The *nobody knows* factor casts doubt on the benefits of business models. Many business schools use case studies to help people understand past successes, but they must be handled with care. It can be difficult to discern the reasons for success and even harder to replicate it. As Phil Rosenzweig's 'halo effect' tells us, much research 'obscures the basic truth that success in the business world is based on decisions made under uncertainty and in the face of factors executives cannot control [and that] personal subjective factors are prominent'.[3] This is especially so in the creative economy due to the personal difference and the importance of novelty. A manager's skill at coping with uncertainty is what counts, which involves making tacit judgements, working with other creative workers and communicating the decision to co-workers.

The fact that intangible value and demand are uncertain puts tremendous pressure on all sides to negotiate deals that minimise the costs (the downside) while trying to retain any possible upside. The most common strategy is to cover the known costs and to seek an increasing share of long-term profit. The seller will want gross profit, while the buyer will try to keep everything within net profit. Success is gained not by the accumulation of capital but by the ability to minimise this uncertainty.

The Network Office

Because of the *personal difference,* many creative people work alone or in small groups, and on a project-by-project basis, using offices and companies when they need to. I have described elsewhere the *network office,* which is best described as a hub of communities.[4] It provides a habitat for the *post-employment job,* the full-time job that is contracted on a self-employed basis; the *just-in-time person,* similar to just-in-time logistics, who seeks to minimise the time spent unemployed, not in the sense of being without a job but in the sense of doing nothing; and the *temporary company,* which is set up to give legal shape to a team of people for a particular project, and which disbands once the project is completed.

In the creative ecology, people use a network of companies to achieve the effects they desire. This is why many well-known and successful creative businesses are smaller than outsiders might expect; they are operating efficiently and effectively as a network office. These hubs look like a point on a Mandelbrot set, as devised by the French mathematician Benoit Mandelbrot, which expresses a fractal shape that is independent of scale. A network office can operate at any scale, since its resources depend not on its own size but on the number of networks it has access to.

Managing a network office requires different skills from managing a hierarchy, especially in how collaboration is managed. In formal organisations, workers can reasonably expect their colleagues to cooperate, if asked. In a network, independent workers frequently have to ask for help from people who are under no obligation to help them. Judging when and how to make such a request is a basic skill. The person approached will be likely to help on the *mutual benefit* principle: if you help me, I'll help you next time. This collaboration is the most common form of relationship in a creative ecology. The results are not necessarily reflected in cheaper inputs but in the long-term benefits to each partner and to the ecology itself.

The network office builds on people's diversity and their interest in collaboration because it is a sensible strategy for achieving a known goal and because it provides a more intense learning experience. During the exchange, individuals may find that mutualism and collaboration bring higher returns in negotiation than would more selfish cost-calculating strategies.

Copyright Is Currency

Copyright, patent, trademark and other intellectual property (IP) rights are best seen as a capital asset that can be created and spent, bought and sold. Creative workers need to know IP rules intimately. Their decision about if, when and how to *claim* an ownership asset and if, when and how to *use* it is a major factor in determining their bargaining power.

Creative workers who follow their *personal priorities* in making expressive works rely mostly on copyright and design rights. They can divide and license their rights in numerous ways according to the right's definition, scope, media, language and term. Each slice has its own revenue potential. Inventors of new ways of making or doing something with a technical effect use patents. Someone who does business under a new name can apply for a trademark. There is a fundamental difference between copyright, patents and trademarks, chiefly because copyright automatically arises when the work is made but patents and trademarks have to be applied for and paid for.

Ideas are non-excludable, in that when I give you an idea I still get to keep it myself. Contracts about IP attempt to square this circle by enabling the sellers to keep as much of the ideas as they can while allowing the buyers to also make money out of them. In effect, the sellers want to retain their right's absolute value, while the buyers want to fragment it and create new value for themselves.

It might seem that the best way to calculate the value of IP is to determine what it cost. However, as we have seen, it is hard to assess the cost of an idea and it is even harder to assess the cost of an idea with added IP protection. The most common method is to estimate the cash flow in future years and then discount back to the present day. Another way is to compare similar assets in the market, known as 'fair value', although it can be difficult to find similar assets in a business where everything has a degree of novelty.

Both seller and buyer have the freedom to arrange whatever licence they wish. In practice, most copyrights are sold in bundles over a period of time, in order to maximise the gains to the seller and reduce administrative costs for both parties. A distributor who owns rights will want to offer the optimal product that is available and affordable. A buyer's preference may be a product that is not available or for which the buyer would pay more but for which the market has no price mechanism. This constrains sellers to play safe, as increasingly evident in bookshops and cinemas. The internet's long tail may increase flexibilities but there is little evidence so far of any significant impact on supply.

Mixed Portfolios

In Chapter 4 it was seen that a mixed-use farm with different ways of handling knowledge is more robust than a monoculture farm with a standardised workforce who all think alike and deal with a smaller number of outside relationships. Having a diverse range of products and relationships has similar benefits for people who are nurturing ideas.

The most obvious benefit of having a larger number of contracts with a diverse range of buyers (a *mixed portfolio*) is to learn more and reduce risk. The major TV, film, music and publishing industries, as well as major manufacturing industries, prefer this kind of strategy. The Hollywood studios each limit output to about twenty films a year, on the basis of their development and production capacities, their competitors' behaviour and the audience capacities since they know the maximum number of films that cinemas (and audiences) can take in one year. Pharmaceutical companies operate similarly to spread the risks involved in R&D.

Using diversity to increase the opportunities for learning is equally important. People benefit by using as wide a variety of people as possible in their own learning process, whether colleagues, competitors, suppliers, customers or complete strangers. This is chiefly due to the serial factor, in that much of their work is never finished and is always open to further adaptation. There is always scope for redefining meaning and identifying demand, not in the hope that one will find the ultimate solution but so that one is able to move the idea on to the next stage and the next contract.

7

The Way Forward

Growing Talent

What is the growth model for an ecology where imagination and learning are more important than physical resources? And how do we get from here to there?

Life is complicated, subtle and delicate, as ecology reminds us. Nothing should be taken for granted. The balance of nature (I almost wrote the 'balance of power') is easily shifted. Small changes in population numbers or inputs of food or energy can lead to expansion or terminal decline. What is growth? Do things always improve, as claimed by founding father Haeckel and biologist Edward Wilson, or is change just as likely to end in a dead-end?

The theory that comes closest is Joseph Schumpeter's *Theory of Economic Development* written when he was living in Austria in 1911. Schumpeter built on Thorstein Veblen's ideas about 'conspicuous consumption' and like him later moved to America to study the phenomenon first-hand. He suggested that economic growth depends not so much on the accumulation of financial capital, as John Stuart Mill had written fifty years earlier, but on entrepreneurship and innovation. He acknowledged that most new ideas would fail or be superseded. In order to create new business, capitalism had to destroy the old, just as a forest fire renews forest ecologies. Its advantage over socialism was not because open markets were better than central commands at allocating resources but because diversity, change and learning are more efficient at innovation.

Schumpeter rejected the classical assumption that supply and demand would always resolve themselves around an equilibrium point. He argued that equilibria were theoretical constructs that never actually occurred in reality. He was more interested in the process of moving from one state to another.

Thirty-five years later, after he had moved to Harvard, Schumpeter wrote *Capitalism, Socialism and Democracy,* in which he said that this kind of entrepreneurial capitalism would inevitably encourage independent rational thought and cost-benefit analysis, and thus produce a critical, intellectual class that would undermine and ultimately destroy it. In this, he agreed with Marx's *Communist Manifesto* and prefigured the German philosopher and musician Theodor Adorno, who wrote *The Culture Industry: Enlightenment as Mass Deception.* Schumpeter believed that capitalism endlessly propagates the seeds of its own destruction. His observations of American bankers and businessmen in the 1930s and 1940s did not persuade him that they were benevolent rulers, and he would undoubtedly be even more sceptical of today's bankers and lenders.

The claims for today's creative ecology rest on Schumpeter's first claim about creative destruction being right and his second claim about hostile intellectuals being wrong. Or, to be more precise, for today's creative workers being different from their twentieth-century predecessors in that the gulf between the thinker and the doer is now crossed by a single step. Creativity and innovation are not tangential sectors standing alongside farming, manufacturing and services but a transformation of existing systems for exchanging knowledge and ideas.

The reawakening of interest in Schumpeter assumes (I believe, correctly) that his intellectuals are today's creative class with mass scope and scale, and found as often inside business as outside. It is possible to go some way towards accepting Schumpeter's view on art and culture, which he believed capitalism infected as strongly as it did everything else, yet without drawing the social conclusions that he did. The essential contribution he made to economics was to point out how capitalism's transient, chaotic nature was a force for change and adaptation.

Sustaining the Ecology

William Baumol, Yale University's eminent historian of economic growth, identifies four types of contemporary capitalism: entrepreneurial capitalism (which is closest to Schumpeter's ideal socialism), corporate capitalism, state capitalism, and oligarchic capitalism. Entrepreneurial capitalism is the most likely to generate growth and prosperity, followed by the corporate kind. Baumol also admires the state-directed capitalism found in France in the 1960s-70s and in Japan in the 1960s-80s, although it failed miserably in Britain at the same time. He says that all countries have a mix that is always changing. America today is a mix of corporate and entrepreneurial systems, while China mixes state and entrepreneurial systems. He draws parallels between America in the 1880s and China today and suggests that America's current tendency towards corporate capitalism is threatening its rate of creativity and innovation.

An economic system that consists entirely of state- or oligarchy-owned resources of land, capital and labour does not prevent *creativity* but it does prevent a *creative ecology*. The truth of the first point can be seen from the achievements of many historic American, Asian, Arab and European civilisations. China's Han Dynasty and early Islam were rigid and closed, but they both generated beautiful and astonishing works of art, design and performance. Imperial China and Arabic Islam were more innovative in technology and engineering than the classical Greeks and Romans who are so much admired by modern Europeans. The dictatorial rulers of Venice, Florence and Rome in the fifteenth and sixteenth centuries who commissioned Donatello, Leonardo da Vinci, Michelangelo, Raphael and Titian thereby facilitated Europe's greatest artistic renaissance for a thousand years. Art critic Richard Morrison says, 'The ruthlessly authoritarian Austro-Hungarian Empire produced Mozart, Haydn, Beethoven, Schubert and Mahler but democratic postwar

Austria has not produced a single composer whose fame has travelled beyond his own front door'.[1]

But although autocracy is no bar to genius or beauty, it does prevent the emergence of a *creative ecology* with scope and scale. It does so by laws to maintain public order, vigorously and sometimes cruelly enforced, and by shutting off the marginal, the dissident and the not-yet-understood.

Growth Models

At the beginning of the twenty-first century we can see that the rich countries have an inclusive approach to Schumpeter's 'creative destruction', mixing art and science, creativity and innovation, in emergent forms. Most of them score highly in diversity, change, learning and the openness of their adaptive processes, as well as having a high level of emergent thinking. In 2008 the rich countries' research organisation, the OECD, met in Korea to spell out some of their ideals. The resulting Seoul Declaration proposed policies 'to maintain an open environment that supports the free flow of information; learning throughout society; wider access to public sector information, including scientific data and cultural heritage; the use of collaborative internet-based models; social networks; and innovative approaches to provide creators and rights-holders with incentives to create and disseminate works in a mutually beneficial way'.[2]

Within this rich countries' group, unsurprisingly, there are differences. In America, creativity and innovation are applied vigorously in all areas of society. Significantly, America has both the world's strongest corporations and the strongest non-profit NGOs in mutually combative, learning and adaptive relationships. In Europe, diversity is more pronounced and change and learning are more variable. In some European countries, the creative ecology is seen as the side-effect of a decline in manufacturing, whether real (Britain) or perceived (Italy), while in Germany and the Nordic countries it is as much part of manufacturing as of the arts. Throughout Europe, government policies are centred on job creation and urban regeneration for the ever-expanding numbers of university graduates who want to live in the cities.

Japan ranks high in cultural strength and technological innovation. Its culture, in the widest sense of that word, is rich, distinctive and robust. The country's postwar strategy, led by the powerful Ministry of International Trade and Industry (MITI), enabled it to recover from military defeat to become the world's second-largest economy, with outstanding innovation in consumer electronics and vehicles producing the world's largest trade surplus by the 1990s. As a result of intensive learning and adaptation, Japan achieved two objectives that might appear incompatible. It understood the West's consumer demands without losing its unique cultural identity. As a result, its style and design are still recognisably distinct, both in sectors that draw directly on Japan's traditional aesthetics, such as clothes and architecture, and in newer sectors, like motor vehicles, where its manufacturers compete successfully with American and German manufacturers. Other Asian countries such as Taiwan, South Korea and Singapore which wanted to be world-class without jeopardising their indigenous culture learned a lot from the Japanese. Japan's weakness is its uniformity. It lacks diversity in ethnic terms and in social attitudes, and its rate of change is slow.

China is unusual in being outside the West's sphere of influence even more than is Japan. Like Japan, it wishes to maintain its unique, rich culture. It also intends to become the world's richest country. It has used its population of 1.3 billion and its very low wage levels to become the world's major exporter of products, from potatoes to iPods. But it has ambitions to do more. It wants to produce the next Apple Inc., not just assemble the iPod's bits and pieces (and it would be quite happy if the potatoes moved to Africa). Its llth Five Year Plan for 2006-2010 gave priority to creativity and innovation and many cities in China are seeking to enhance their population's creative skills. China is determined to change, learn and adapt, although it is equally determined to learn on its own terms. Its main vulnerability is its dislike of diversity, perhaps matched by the current shortness of creative talent, but its creative ecology has grown faster than any other country's, ever.

China's textile manufacturers show the country's lack of diversity and the problems of adaptation. They grew rapidly through the 1990s by undercutting other exporters and in 2006 brought in 20 per cent of the country's total export earnings. However, they soon faced rapid wage inflation, a high-valued Chinese renminbi and a weak American dollar. The Dubai traders who buy most of China's textiles on behalf of America and Europe so as to avoid EU and American quotas began to look elsewhere in Asia. The Chinese quickly had to upgrade their quality standards and work more closely with retailers. They found this difficult, because they lacked the diverse skills and the knowledge that were required. Their learning capacity was not strong enough.

Most *rural developing countries* find it hard to change or to learn. They lack a strong tradition of independent thinking, a strong arts sector, or a strong business community that could provide a springboard. Their diversity is as likely to lead to tribal conflict as creative achievement. They are hampered by high population growth rates (except China), a large agricultural sector, low GNP per capita, patchy education, a low capital-labour ratio, regressive bureaucracies and poor infrastructure. Many elites have high levels of corruption, which are debilitating for everyone outside the elite but which militate especially against independent and often powerless creative workers.

India will overtake China as the world's most populous country by 2020. It has a profound culture, a high level of education and significant business skills, but its creative exports are relatively low. Its rich heritage in music, dance and costume is held back by feudal village rules and a caste system that prevents many performers from earning a living wage and results in high suicide rates.[3] However, its middle-class schoolchildren learn computer programming earlier than do American children and have equal if not higher pass rates; and innovation initiatives like the Gujarat-based Honey Bee Network achieve a level of knowledge-sharing with a transparency and efficiency that many Western networks might envy.

Brazil has a similar mix of a deep, vibrant culture, extensive poverty and a rich upper class. It has outstanding skills in design, music and sport. Culture minister Gilberto Gil enthusiastically applied new ideas in education, digital media and design, and the country is a leader in the commercial use of biofuels. But many of Gil's government colleagues and most of the private sector that has fuelled Brazil's economic boom since 2000 still regard culture as marginal and unbusiness-like. Given a choice in Brazil and India between funding basic social infrastructure and funding culture it is hard to argue for the latter. Yet without a creative ecology where children and young people can learn, development will be slower and more dependent on external influences.

There is a close correlation between a country's poverty and its level of knowledge.[4] The United Nations Conference on Trade and Development (UNCTAD) has produced two world maps showing a poverty gap and a knowledge gap between the best and the worst. A map of a *creativity gap* shows the same disturbing picture.

It is not easy to break out of the circle of deprivation. These poorer countries fear diversity and are pessimistic about change. They do not see how to get on the ladder of adaptation. Some have become the outsourced back-rooms of richer Western economies and of China and India. There are some signs of change. Some countries are working hard to build their arts and culture domains. The American LightYearsIP company is working with Ethiopia and other African countries to use intellectual property to increase the value of exports and thereby reduce poverty.[5] The continuously evolving *Atlas of Ideas* monitors innovation worldwide. But there is a long way to go. Creative value can only be added through people's imagination, skilled talent and personal judgement, and often comes with a high price-ticket, not unskilled low-cost labour.

East and West

Working in London and Shanghai, I am often asked if Western traditions of creativity and innovation are the best or even the only way to support creative ecologies, as many in the West assume, or if Asian ways are better, as China and Japan believe. Do Europe's and America's creative ecologies have unique advantages? Or, to turn the question around, does Asia have advantages that the West lacks? To what extent is the West's rapid growth dependent on its cultural contexts, regulatory structures and free markets in capital and labour? Are the two models transposable?

The two archetypes are profoundly different. Western companies emphasise the novelty of what is produced and use 'breakthrough' and 'disruption' as words of praise. The social after-effects are assumed to be beneficial and are left to the marketplace. In contrast, China starts with its belief in a harmonious society and allows creativity and innovation only if it can be shown to strengthen society. Of course, these descriptions are caricatures. There are many in the West who share Asian views on collaboration, such as the Free and Open Source Software community (though FOSS people rightly despair at China's restrictions on free speech). And there are growing numbers of people in China who admire the selfish shocks and competition of Western business.

There are some signs of change on both sides. The new generation of Chinese have different attitudes and ambitions from their parents'. (Chinese universities will produce about 84 million graduates between 2000 and 2015.) They are increasingly confident and articulate about their sense of individual identity. They are growing up in a world where online collaboration is the norm, in spite of government censorship. And Chinese companies are unlikely to turn their backs on this generation, as a source of ideas, as exemplars of a new way of working or as customers for their products. Meanwhile, in the West, the allure of China as the next world superpower means that the number of visitors to China grows every year and the scale of the symbiosis and collaboration between China and the rest of the world grows too. Finally, there is the growing awareness in Brussels and Beijing and even in Washington, DC, that banking, energy and pollution and other major issues facing us today cannot be resolved without joint action on the basis of common understanding engendered through conversation and dialogue.

The Tipping Point

When does a network of creative people become a fully fledged ecology? Is there a tipping point? The best indicators of scale are the quality of diversity, change, learning and adaptation: when personal expression, ideas, images and symbols come to the forefront of people's concerns. But these are hard to quantify. So we must rely on easier, quantitative methods of the relative sizes of the manufacturing, service and creative sectors, although, as I hope is clear, it is increasingly difficult to tell them apart.

To get *scope,* the ecology will also have stability (no earthquakes, civil conflicts or wars), a high level of smart demand, a high level of business acumen, inventiveness and risk-taking, and an intellectual property framework that supports creativity and innovation. To get *scale* as well, it will have a world language and a media culture with characters, stories, TV, film and fashion that are globally desired.

8

New Places, New Policies

Creativity Is Not Deferential

Even enlightened governments find it difficult to understand and make policies for a creative ecology. Is it possible to regulate diversity and novelty? Michael Batty, Director of London's Centre for Advanced Spatial Analysis (CASA), says that creative cities are in the vanguard of 'chaos, non-linearity, disruptive technologies, emergence and surprise'.[1] No ordinary politician would welcome such a task.

A government's job is to know and control, but creativity is often not knowable and never controllable. Governments that are accustomed to financing large-scale infrastructure projects have difficulty in understanding individuals and companies that are small-scale and whose meanings, outputs and values are uncertain. Politicians can finance a school, but they cannot order up a new idea. They can control the hard factors of power, but it is hard to influence the soft infrastructure. Indeed, a self-organising system often regards an outside instruction as hostile and to be worked around.

A visit to Berlin reveals the difference. The transgressive, dangerous Berlin of the 1920s, with its world-class Bauhaus design, Fritz Lang's films, outstanding painters and cartoonists and Kurt Weill's music and cabaret, as well as the philosophy and writings of CJ. Jung and Walter Benjamin, has gone forever, unlikely to resurface or, if it did, be welcomed. Today, twenty years after the Wall came down, Berlin is once again a likeable city, but it looks unlikely to match its disorderly predecessor in diversity, genius or impact. The city's manifesto for European Cities in Creativity makes several good points, including creativity as a force for structural change, economic growth and employment, and culture as a force for attractiveness. All true, but not enough.

The decision by a government to support culture comes at a cost. The Berlin city government is much prouder of today's city than its predecessors were of the 1920s version, but the result is an increase in uniformity and compliance. The creative ecology requires new policies, but new ways of working are often held back by old ways of governing.

Yet the briefest look at the world's successful creative ecologies in America, Europe and Japan shows that regulations are critically important. As a creative ecology starts to grow, regulations become more important, either as support or as hindrance. Chen Qingtai, of China State Council's Development Centre, says, 'the market is the development space, and policy is the development boundary'.[2]

The boundaries are being forever pushed outwards. Regulations can be divided into two categories: general laws of the land, which affect everyone, and sector-specific laws for particular markets. As creative ecologies spread, there is a universal trend from the particular to the general, as laws that used to apply only to specialists become applicable to the whole population. For example, copyright, which originally affected only professional authors, now affects almost everyone.

How laws are made is as important as the laws themselves. I am tempted to say that the process is even more important than the policy. It would be nice to produce perfect policies every time, but this seldom happens, and even the most perfect policy becomes imperfect over time. Most regulation is a response to market failure, and, as regulations are imposed and businesses respond, so the nature of the market failure changes. Regulation is seldom a zero sum game.

Successful policies can only grow out of collaboration between government and business to ensure that, when they are implemented, they are appropriate and that, as new situations arise, so new regulations are prepared. The evidence shows that government and business need to work in tandem. The role of Japan's Ministry of International Trade and Investment (MITI) from 1949 through to the 1980s can hardly be overestimated, and the Canadian Department of Communications was similarly successful in the early 1990s.

Since bad regulations can do as much damage as good regulations do benefit, the European Commission and many European governments have adopted tests for good regulations that all new proposals must pass. The main criteria are: interdisciplinary, transparent, evidence-based, consultative, and proportionate. The tests are voluntary and not always followed. Perhaps governments should add another criterion: implementation.

A Policy Audit

Governments that want a creative ecology will carry out a *policy audit* on their laws and regulations to ensure they are fit for the ecology. Policy audits are similar to a financial audit for a company's accounts or an environmental audit to assess a policy's impact on the environment. Many laws set up to address the needs of a manufacturing economy are inappropriate for a creative ecology. The laws on intellectual property are an obvious example. There are many others. The British government sensibly updated its rules on payments to unemployed people to acknowledge that young musicians would prefer to work unpaid at a music-related job than to work and be paid for the wrong kind of job. There are few typologies for a policy audit (my Shanghai report proposed a framework for China). I will give three examples: learning, copyright and international trade.

Learning to Learn

Given the interdependence of learning and creativity, as well as the high proportion of graduates in creative occupations, it is not surprising that governments emphasise education as a motivational instrument of creative ecologies. It helps, too, that they control the provision of education, whereas, as we have seen, they have less influence over people's inclination to receive it. A government controls education chiefly by controlling the annual budget and the curriculum. Through the budget, it decides almost everything: from primary teachers' take-home pay to whether the school roof is repaired this year to university students' fees. By controlling the curriculum, it regulates whether creative thinking should be encouraged in all subjects or restricted to art and so-called creative writing, as is more often the case. The balance between centralised instruction, in which people must strive to give the correct answers, and liberal learning, in which people think for themselves, is a difficult one to get right.

And yet these structural factors provide only a skeleton and ignore, as it were, the living tissue of the learning process. For this, we need to treat education as a potential learning system. We can ensure that education systems meet the local community's needs for knowledge and learning; support open universities that enable people of any age to learn what they want, when they want; encourage universities to make their libraries open to the public; encourage international exchanges (more important for smaller countries); bring think-tanks, research bodies and NGOs into the education process; bring children's own skills into school (many teachers believe that video games are harmful even when children show extraordinary ability at them); and protect learning-for-the-sake-of-learning from being squeezed out by learning-for-a-job vocational courses *(thinking is a proper job)*.

We can use policies to finance libraries and multimedia centres; divert the public R&D budget into growth areas with spin-out effects on neighbouring activities (in practice, most public R&D budgets go into massive industrial silos like aerospace and pharmaceuticals); use R&D grants and tax credits to mitigate risk in all sectors that are creative and innovative (in practice, most R&D schemes only help innovation); increase the ways that individuals, businesses and universities can cross-fertilise their learning activities (sometimes called 'knowledge transfer'); and provide subsidies for adult courses that are easily understood and easy to use (many countries have subsidies but few pass my two tests of access).

Learning depends on a free flow of information and so a creative ecology will also have laws on intellectual property that assist this flow.

Balancing Ownership and Access

A creative ecology needs inherited ideas as much, if not more, than it needs inherited financial capital, in order to sustain diversity. Creative people want to be free to use ideas from the past and from their contemporaries. The laws on copyright and patents specify who owns what and who has access to it. They have the power to increase or decrease the flow of ideas by controlling how we get access to ideas, how we share ideas and how we make money out of ideas.

The purpose of intellectual property was clearly stated in the first copyright law passed by the English parliament in 1709, titled 'An Act for the Encouragement of Learning', and by the American constitutional commitment that says its laws should serve progress: it is to enhance the flow of ideas. The laws do that by protecting upfront investment and allowing investors and owners to limit usage while also specifying where access is allowed. They have to balance the restrictions of ownership against the benefits of access. No law gets the balance perfectly right, but some try harder than others.

On the one hand, rights-holders want their rights to be as

strong as possible and to last as long as possible so they can protect their investment and earn the maximum revenues from current outlets as well as keeping options open for the future. The film and music industries have benefited enormously from Japan's R&D in recording technology, enabling them to license their rights on DVD and other platforms not invented when the material was originally produced.

But a creative ecology also needs access. So others argue that the laws have become too strong and that the costs to society may outweigh the benefits to rights-holders. In the 1980s the creators of Free and Open Source Software (FOSS) developed a General Public Licence (GPL) to allow other people to adapt their software freely, on the condition that they subsequently allow others the same freedoms. More recently, Creative Commons (CC) licences encourage people to use digital media. These access-reformers also want more fundamental change. The Access to Knowledge (A2K) movement seeks to leverage knowledge to promote learning, to enhance individuals' participation in community and cultural affairs, to protect human rights and freedoms, to protect and preserve the public domain, and to create opportunities for people to participate in the creation of knowledge. This last aim is particularly valuable, as it affirms the collaborative nature of learning. The Adelphi Charter on Creativity, Innovation and Intellectual Property is part of this movement, laying out fair, balanced principles for a creative ecology.

The intellectual property laws that were devised for the repetitive economy are unsuitable for a creative ecology. So far, however, most governments have found it difficult to revise them. There seems to be an in-built reluctance to do research or to accept the research that is done. Governments apply the principles of good regulation to intellectual property significantly less often than they do in other areas of regulation. In 2006, as a result of the Gowers committee on copyright, Britain became one of the few European countries to use independent research as a basis for policy, and France is similarly reasonable, but the European Commission continues to be erratic in its treatment of evidence. Intellectual property laws could be a powerful means of promoting access to knowledge and to learning. Too often, the opposite is true.

Trading Ideas

Trade barriers increase the prices of imports, or ban them altogether, which protects local producers and may increase local employment but also increases costs. Although all members of the World Trade Organisation (WTO) are committed to dismantling barriers, they all reserve the right to keep them if they want to. Progress depends on a member deciding that by dismantling its barrier A it will encourage other members to dismantle their barrier B.

History shows that countries support free trade when they are strong enough to be net exporters. When Britain and America were agricultural societies, they banned food imports. When they were industrialising, they had high tariffs, and American copyright rules covered only domestic books until as recently as 1954. But the recent picture is more muddled. Both Europe and America espouse free trade in most sectors but they still vigorously protect their farmers, and Europe also protects its culture from American imports. Japan benefits by keeping its barriers, and a survey of post-1950s development in Latin America, Africa and Asia, and of the Eastern European countries that joined the European Union after 1990, shows mixed results.

Should a country use trade regulations to protect its creative ecology? Imports are a source of diversity, but too many can dilute local cultures. We can start by saying that in principle all national ecologies should be open and free, but we can also acknowledge that, if trade is imbalanced, countries may reasonably want to protect their own ecosystems. They may do so through price discrimination of state education, especially at university level; discrimination between domestic and foreign workers; content quotas for TV broadcasts and cinema films; restricting subsidies to nationals; and so on. These can and do work, as seen in countries as varied as Britain, Brazil and South Korea. But there are conditions. First, the government has to be sensitive to temporary inequalities and adept at managing them through subsidies, cheap credit and so on. Second, it has to learn how to fill the gap by either indigenous resources or carefully managed foreign resources. In Asia, both Japan and Korea had such resources. Without them, trade barriers can condemn a country to treading water, at best.

9

Three Steps to Growth

Thinking Is a Proper Job

The new ecology and its dramatic scope and scale can be summarised in three principles: 'Everyone is creative', 'Creativity needs freedom' and 'Freedom needs markets'.

'Everyone Is Creative'

Creativity is a defining characteristic of homo sapiens. The capacity to be creative is something we are all born with. Knowing is an indicator of life, and thinking, which is being self-conscious about knowing, is an indicator of creativity. We all have a *creative instinct,* hard-wired and genetically inherited in the same way as the language instinct identified by Noam Chomsky and Steven Pinker.[1]

This creative instinct is not the exclusive prerogative of

people doing a special job, such as artists or inventors, or of people with extraordinary talent, such as geniuses or experts. We are all creative in the sense of imagining alternatives and in our desire to change and improve our surroundings. We are creative whenever we act on our desire to create beauty.

In saying that the creative instinct is deeply personal and private we may deny ourselves the validity of generalising about it. Joseph Brodsky admitted as much in his acceptance speech to the Nobel Foundation in 1987, and he went on to say that he wanted to explain what this meant:

> If art teaches anything (to the artist, in the first place), it is the privateness of the human condition. Being the most ancient as well as the most literal form of private enterprise, it fosters in a man, knowingly or unwittingly, a sense of his uniqueness, of individuality, of separate-ness - thus turning him from a social animal into a perceptible 'I.' Lots of things can be shared: a bed, a piece of bread, convictions, a mistress - but not a poem by, say, Rainer Maria Rilke.[2]

One winces at Brodsky's mention of mistresses, but he was speaking in the 1980s and it did not stop America appointing him Poet Laureate a few years later. He is right to admit the personal and private and also to acknowledge the need to talk about it.

It starts young. Watch as children learn and develop how to move, dress, speak, understand, assert and express themselves. Adults who say they are not creative have simply lost the ability to be children. Jean Piaget, who trained as a zoologist (he loved snails), pioneered the idea that intelligence is not inherited but actively created by a child's interaction with his or her surroundings. Children learn by being creative. Childhood expert Tina Bruce says children develop along three dimensions: the emergent beginnings of creativity, the process of developing a creative thought (being creative), and making creative products.[3] When we feel nostalgic for childhood, we are remembering this joy of learning and self-discovery. Of course, while everyone can be creative, every population contains people who only exercise their creative instinct when young and thereafter become incurious and uncreative.

A good indicator of latent creativity leading to adaptive behaviour is when people answer 'Yes' to these 'dreaming' questions:

- Do you dream, and do you have fantasies?
- Do you think about how things might be *different?*
- Do you often think of a *better* way of doing something?
- Do you *want* to think of a better way?
- Do you take pride in doing things *your way?*
- Do you like to make things more *beautiful?*

Saying that 'everyone is creative' does not mean 'everyone is talented'. That would be like saying that everyone who can walk can be a professional athlete or anyone who can write can write a best-selling novel. Talent implies exceptional ability with a dose of hard work and a sprinkling of luck. Indeed, talent is rare in children and an exceptional amount of it seems slightly spooky.

Nor does the principle deny the importance of collaboration. It is often misunderstood to mean that collaboration is secondary, even second-rate. The opposite is just as likely to be true. Collaboration flourishes because individuals wish it so. Enforced collaboration is hardly worth the game.

People often disagree about the relationship between the individual and the group in the creative process. It is often seen as an either/or choice between personal expression and group collaboration. At one extreme, there is the sanctity of personal expression. At the other, groups and corporations that put a premium on stability and routine find it scary when people work on their own and believe that ideas produced outside the group will not be as good as those produced inside the group. Many ideas bounce through the two extremes. Indeed, the ecology is a continual process of adaptation between the individual and the environment.

Thinking is the piston of creativity. Creative workers need to be continually on the alert to pick up new ideas (*be a magpie*). They need to know whether what they think is new really is new, to know what it means, and to negotiate the best terms. A defining characteristic of creative people is the dedication they give to thinking about their work; it is a barrier to entry by casual or half-hearted people. Creativity is extremely competitive in terms of the quality of what is created and may well be more competitive than routine, repetitive activities, although there is little data on this.

It is one of the basic characteristics of creative work that it is individually driven and individually sized and even leading companies can be small-scale in business terms. You cannot start a small-scale steel mill, but you can think for yourself. Thinking is a proper job.

The creative economy may be the first economy to pivot

on an individual rather than groups, at least since the days of hunting and gathering, and the first to celebrate the individual as individual. The individual replaces the firm or organisation as the main actor, player, stakeholder and decision-maker.

'Creativity Needs Freedom'

It is true that some remarkable work has been created in prison or in totalitarian societies, but, if people's latent creativity is to flourish with scale and scope, people need to inhabit niches where they feel at home and free to do their best work (the two are obviously related) and are stimulated by the external environment. In such places, they feel comfortable and feel free to be creative. It is expected of them, or, at least, novelty and the unexpected will not be frowned upon.

A creative ecology needs freedom *from* and freedom *to*. It needs freedom from constraints such as physical want, hunger, prejudice, censorship and unhelpful education systems. It needs freedom to in the sense of freedom of expression and freedom of communication. It flourishes best where people think their own thoughts and challenge conventional wisdom about the quality or the relevance of other people's ideas. Free expression is a condition of creativity (as creativity empowers freedom), although what matters most is not speech but the freedom to question, subvert and reinvent one's *relationship to an idea.*

Our autonomy pivots on our ability to manage this relationship. In a creative ecology, we are free to take in new ideas, think about them, reconfigure them, play with them, and then to either reject them or relaunch them in new shapes and forms. We are free to handle abstract thoughts, explore new concepts, operate across topic boundaries and wander into new areas. Above all, we are free to trust our own perceptions. This requires an ability to maintain cognitive diversity (keeping two ideas going at the same time) without collapsing into cognitive dissonance (becoming schizoid as a result). Rejection is as important as relaunching. The mark of a creative mind is as much its ability to get rid of old ideas as it is to embrace new ones. There is nothing worse than being seduced by an idea that should be junked.

Autonomy cannot exist on a large scale unless it is acceptable and deeply held throughout society: across all groups, within families and between generations. A creative ecology accepts each individual's claim to build up his or her creative capital and accepts that it has commercial value. According to classical economics, financial capital consists of assets that are used for future purposes and can be made, inherited or borrowed. How much more important it is to generate, inherit and borrow ideas, and to do so freely.

Being socially acceptable implies that it is acceptable to fail (regrettable but acceptable), because failure can be a useful stepping-stone on the way to success. Of course, we prefer to win, but we know we may fail. The trick is to see failure as a device for learning. This acceptance is part of tolerance in general.

This freedom, if it means anything, must allow the disturbing and shocking to occur. Vibrant cultures allow a role for this, like the Trickster in North American cultures, the Fools, Jesters and Jokers in medieval Europe, the Middle East's Nasruddin, China's Monkey King and the artist and comedian today. These people play with us, mocking our status, gender roles, beliefs and manners. They are licensed to embarrass us.

The relationship between private thoughts and public expression can be a valuable source of meaning, but it can also lead to tension. Some people are comfortable expressing their own personality and identity, while others find it embarrassing. Americans are probably the most open and Asians the least open. New Yorkers love talking about their private lives to anyone within hearing (amply demonstrated by the success of *Friends* and *Sex and the City*), but Asians think private lives should stay private. So this private/public nexus favours some cultures and not others in supporting change, diversity and adaptation.

'Freedom Needs Markets'

The first two principles relate to the mind and how it functions. The third principle is concerned with 'out-there' interaction. If we want to follow our ideas through, we need places where we can exchange ideas in a mutual traffic and where other people can put a value on them. In this sense, freedom is a primary tool that enables one to use other tools such as technology and money.

What is the basic exchange unit of creativity and innovation? Are ideas essentially different from other resources, other currencies? They are certainly non-rivalrous: I can give you an idea without losing it myself. They are therefore more easily shared. Are they different in other ways? How does a market in ideas actually operate?

A market of some sort is a necessary condition for economic activity. It tests value, usually through allocating resources, and by setting prices. An efficient market enhances the sharing and reuse of information, whether a transaction takes place or not; it allows people to know about each other's preferences; it brings together buyers and sellers (or users); and it resolves demand and supply curves around optimal pricing.

Markets have historically been places where information is exchanged, sometimes as a precursor to a transaction and sometimes for its own sake. It is often difficult, in advance, to differentiate the two. Many economists have developed theories about information markets, notably Hal Varian, George Akerlof and Michael Spence, but their theories focus on the exchange of fixed data rather than the more dynamic process of creating new ideas. Robert Metcalfe's formula suggests that the value of a network depends on how many people use it. It is much harder to estimate how they use it.

The history of economic growth since 1950 shows a strong correlation between open markets and creative ecologies. Without markets, creativity might flourish but a creative economy could not. Countries with a totalitarian or command economy, such as the USSR and Warsaw Pact countries 1945-90, prevented people from developing and sharing their ideas, let alone setting up businesses. As a result, the Soviet countries found it difficult to work in an innovative, multi-disciplinary manner across different sectors. Innovation was treated as a specialist case rather than being encouraged as a general principle. Data was used to support government policies rather than being available to all to help their own investigations and explorations. There were few independent intermediaries. People were not encouraged to think for themselves.[4]

Creativity needs an indefinitely large number of market-places. It needs *social marketplaces* that enable us to know what is going on, to exchange ideas, to enquire, to check the truth of what is happening, to explore our own paths. In these markets, price is not the only nexus. Maslow's needs are equally if not more influential. Creativity also needs *commercial markets* where we can put our ideas on sale to gain commercial value and create wealth. Ideas are intangible and their price is thoroughly elastic. The exchange of ideas has low resource costs and low transactional costs, as well as very fast transactional speeds of distribution, feedback and response. The freedom to create a new market is as important as the freedom to create a new product.

A Model Ecology

The internet dramatically validates these three principles of the creative ecology: the awareness that creativity is universal, the freedom to exercise it, and the ease with which markets can be set up. It has spawned new social networks that recognise and celebrate the latent need to create and make a virtue of being open and inclusive and thereby enhance the network's diversity.

The sheer quantity of ideas 'in the air' is far too much for anyone to comprehend, which is as it should be.

10

The New Billion

Looking for a Job

The creative ecology is part of the evolution of open societies. It is marked by the recognition that everyone has their own creative characteristics and that these characteristics need freedom and markets if they are to be expressed, shared and acted upon. The result is an increase in adaptive learning systems and a higher rate of social development.

The high rates of diversity, change, learning and adaptation mean that at any one moment many people are out of step with the rest of the population, if temporarily. Equilibrium may be a useful theoretical construct but it is seldom achieved and never for long. Some see this as liberating and productive, others as worrying and distressing.

There will always be a tension between private creativity

and the public transactions that result, between the individual and the group, and between freedom and regulation. Different cultures and different mindsets treat this in different ways.

Every few years, a billion young people are looking for their first job *(thinking is a proper job)*. Many are young, hardly teenagers, and will do what their parents do, working in the fields or behind a counter, helping out. Others continue at school, looking for a job when they are teenagers, while a small percentage go to university and start looking for a job when they are in their twenties. I call these young people the *new billion.*

What do they want to do? Where do they want to go? To learn? To work? To live? To fall in love? As they get older, many will have more freedom and be faced with more choices. An increasing proportion of those with education, cash and confidence will move to mix with different people, places and spaces. Those in the countryside who can will move to the city. Very few will move in the opposite direction, to the countryside.

These new nomads will determine the shape and vigour of their local niches, not only for themselves but for others. In major cities they will become part of the 20-30 per cent of the population that is foreign-born. They are by definition diverse and they are likely to be challenging, in the same way that Europeans arriving in Philadelphia and New York in the nineteenth century were challenging. They are on their own and they need to ask questions and work hard to get ahead.

This is exciting for them and a source of pride to their parents and teachers as well as to their country. But which country? These nomads may have negative effects on the places they leave, depending on where they go and how long they stay away. Most cities regard population growth and increased diversity as virtues, and want to attract more bright, young, talented foreigners. European universities, facing a shortfall in local applicants, are actively recruiting foreigners from Asia. These migration patterns both between and inside countries are a source of concern to many countries.

Everyone has to do it his or her way. We are only individuals trying to make the best of our surroundings, whatever lies around us: making sense, trying to improve, searching for beauty and elegance. It is hard to do this on one's own.

Notes

Chapter 1: The Challenge

1. *Complete Letters of Vincent Van Gogh* (1978), Thames & Hudson, London, p. 13.
2. *Complete letters of Vincent Van Gogh,* p. 184.
3. John Carey (2006), *What Good Are the Arts?,* Faber & Faber, London.
4. Alan Heeks (2000), *The Natural Advantage,* Nicholas Brealey, London.
5. For example, Nathaniel Southgate Shaler, often described as the founder of American geology, in *Nature and Man in America,* Scribner's, 1895.
6. John Howkins (2001), *The Creative Economy,* Penguin, London.
7. John Howkins (2001), *The Creative Economy,* Penguin, London.
8. Joseph Schumpeter (1943), *Capitalism, Socialism and Democracy,* Allen & Unwin, London.

Chapter 2: First Ideas

1. Tony Blair in the *Guardian, 22* July 1997.
2. Tina Bruce (2004), *Cultivating Creativity,* Hodder & Stoughton.
3. Peter Higgs & others (2008), *Beyond the Creative Industries,* NESTA (National Endowment for Science and Technology and the Arts), London.

4. Stuart Cunningham (2006), *What Price a Creative Economy?*, Platform Papers, no. 9.
5. DCMS (2004), 'Evidence Toolkit'.
6. New England Foundation for the Arts (2007), *The Creative Economy: A New Definition*, NEFA.
7. <www.keanet.eu/ecoculturepage.html>.
8. Helen Trinca & Catherine Fox (2004), *Better than Sex*, Random House.
9. John Nightingale & Jason Potts, 'An alternative framework for economies', *Post-Autistic Economics Review*, no. 10, December 2001.
10. Alfred Korzybski (1933, 1995), *Science and Sanity*, Institute of General Semantics.
11. David Bohm (1998), *On Creativity*, Routledge, London.

Chapter 3: Scope and Scale

1. Rolf Jensen (1999), *The Dream Society*, McGraw-Hill; Joseph Pine & James Gilmore (1999), *The Experience Economy*, Harvard Business School, Boston; and Michael J. Wolf (1999), *The Entertainment Economy*, Times Books, New York.
2. The Adelphi Charter on Creativity, Innovation and Intellectual Property (2005). See <www.adelphicharter.org>.
3. Rebecca Harding (2008), *The Future Face of Enterprise*, DEMOS, London.
4. Scott Beardsley, Bradford Johnson & James Manyika (2006), 'Competitive advantage from better interactions', *McKinsey Quarterly*, no. 2.
5. Howard Gardner, 'Breakthrough ideas for 2006', *Harvard Business Review*, February 2006.
6. Richard Caves (2001), *Creative Industries: Contracts between Art and Commerce*, Harvard University Press, Boston.
7. Creative and Skills Council, 2006.

Chapter 4: The Adaptive Mind

1. Fritjof Capra (1996), *The Web of Life*, HarperCollins.
2. Lindemann called them 'trophic' levels (from *trophe*, Greek for 'food').
3. David Bohm (1998), *On Creativity*, Routledge, London.

4. Alan Heeks (2000), *Renewing Yourself,* Nicholas Brealey, London.
5. Richard Dawkins (2003), A *Devil's Chaplain,* Weidenfeld & Nicolson, London.
6. Stephen Jay Gould (1979), *The Spandrels of San Marco and the Panglossian Paradigm,* Royal Society of London, 205.
7. *Complete Letters of Vincent Van Gogh* (1978), Thames & Hudson, London, p. 597.
8. Soedjatmoko (1978), 'The Future and the Learning Capacity of Nations', IIC.
9. Martin Yarnit (ed.) (2007), *Advancing Opportunity: New Models of Schooling,* Smith Institute.
10. Edward Vul & Harold Pashler (2008), *The Crowd Within,* Department of Brain and Cognitive Science, MIT.
11. This is based on a similar example in Richard Dawkins (200?), A *Devil's Chaplain,* Weidenfeld & Nicolson, London.
12. Lawrence Lessig (2000), *Code and Other Laws of Cyberspace,* Basic Books.
13. Etienne Wenger (1996), *Communities of Practice,* Cambridge University Press, Cambridge.
14. C.P. Snow, Rede Lecture, 7 May 1959.
15. John Howkins & Zhao Li (2008), 'Dutty's Dare' ['遭遇创意队'], Xue Lin [学林出版社].
16. Charles Leadbeater (2008), *We-Think: The Power of Mass Creativity,* Profile.
17. Rabindranath Tagore (1970), *Gitanjali,* Macmillan.
18. Robert Macintosh (1992), 'Competition: Historical perspectives', in Evelyn Fox Keller, *Keywords in Evolutionary Biology,* Harvard University Press.
19. Fritjof Capra (1996), *The Web of Life,* HarperCollins.
20. David Bohm (1998), *On Creativity,* Routledge, London.
21. Satish Kumar, Editorial, *Resurgence,* May 2008.

Chapter 5: Creative Places

1. Francis Cook (1 977), *Hua-Yen Buddhism: The Jewel Net of Indra,* Penn State Press.
2. Ulrich Hilpert (1992), 'Archipelago Europe: Islands of innovation', European Commission.

3. Charles Landry & Franco Bianchini (1995), *The Creative City,* DEMOS, London.
4. Cedric Price (1965), Plan for Potteries ThinkBelt.
5. Richard Florida (2001), *The Rise of the Creative Class,* Basic Books.
6. *Monocle,* August 2008.
7. Peter Hall (2001), *Cities in Civilisation,* Fromm.
8. London Development Agency (2008), *London: A Cultural Audit,* LDA.
9. Jane Jacobs (1985), *Cities and the Wealth of Nations,* Viking.
10. Elizabeth Currid (2007), *The Warhol Economy,* Princeton University Press, Princeton.
11. Jaime Lerner (2003), 'Acupuntura urbana', *Editora Record.*
12. <www.w3.org/History/1989/proposal.html>.
13. Yochai Benkler (2006), *The Wealth of Networks,* Yale University Press, New Haven.
14. <www.cluetrain.com>.
15. Eric von Hippel (1995), *The Sources of Innovation,* Oxford University Press, Oxford.
16. Don Tapscott & Anthony D. Williams (2007), *Wikinomics: How Mass Collaboration Changes Everything,* Atlantic Books.

Chapter 6: Negotiating Uncertainty

1. Charlie Tims & Shelagh Wright (2007), *'So, What Do You Actually Do?',* DEMOS, London.
2. Charles Leadbeater (1999), *Living on Thin Air: The New Economy,* Viking, London.
3. Phil Rosenzweig (2009), *The Halo Effect,* Free Press, New York.
4. John Howkins (2001), *The Creative Economy,* Penguin.

Chapter 7: The Way Forward

1. NESTA 02, September 2002.
2. OECD, press release, 18 June 2008.
3. Rustom Bharucha (2003), *Rajasthan: An Oral History,* Penguin.
4. World Bank, World Development Report, 2008.
5. LightYearsIP (2008), *Distinctive Values in African Exports.*

Chapter 8: New Places, New Policies

1. Michael Batty (2007), 'Complexity in city systems', CASA Working Paper 117, UCL, London.
2. *China Daily,* 19 October 2007.

Chapter 9: Three Steps to Growth

1. Stephen Pinker (1995), *The Language Instinct,* Penguin.
2. Nobel Foundation, press release, 1987.
3. Tina Bruce (2004), *Cultivating Creativity,* Hodder & Stoughton.
4. Rex Malik, 'Can the USSR survive 1984?', *InterMedia,* vol. 12, no. 3, May 1984.

Acknowledgements

1. Francis Fukuyama (1993), *The End of History and the Last Man,* Penguin.

References

Abrams, Jan & Peter Hall (eds) (2005), *Else/Where: Mapping. New Cartographies of Networks and Territories,* University of Minnesota.

Adelphi Charter on Creativity, Innovation and Intellectual Property (2005), <www.adelphicharter.org>.

Banham, Reyner (1990), Los *Angeles: The Architecture of Four Ecologies,* Penguin, New York.

Barron, Frank X. (2006), *No Rootless Flower: An Ecology of Creativity,* Hampton Press, Cresskill, NJ.

Batty, Michael (2007), *Cities and Complexity,* MIT Press, Cambridge.

Batty, Michael (2007), 'Complexity in city systems: Understanding, evolution, and design', CASA Working Paper 117, UCL, London.

Baumol, William J. (2007), *Good Capitalism, Bad Capitalism, and the Economics of Growth and Prosperity,* Yale University Press, New Haven.

Beardsley, Scott, Bradford Johnson & James Manyika (2006), 'Competitive advantage from better interactions', *McKinsey Quarterly,* no. 2 (and see same authors, *McKinsey Quarterly,* 2005, no. 4).

Benkler, Yochai (2006), *The Wealth of Networks: How Social Production Transforms Markets and Freedom,* Yale University Press, New Haven.

Benyus, Janine (1997), *Biomimicry: Innovation Inspired by Nature,* William Morrow.

Boden, Margaret (2004), *The Creative Myth,* Routledge, London.

145

Breuer, Georg (1982), *Sociobiology and the Human Dimension,* Cambridge University Press, Cambridge.

Bridgstock, Ruth (2008), *'Follow Your Bliss' or 'Show Me the Money'? Career Orientations, Career Management Competence and Career Success in Australian Creative Workers,* Norwich Business School.

Buck, Nick, and others (2005), *Changing Cities,* Palgrave, London.

Burdett, Ricky & Deyan Sudjic (2007), *The Endless City,* Phaidon, London.

Caves, Richard E. (2001), *Creative Industries: Contracts between Art and Commerce,* Harvard University Press, Cambridge.

Claxton, Guy (2001), *Wise Up: Learning to Live the Learning Life,* Network Educational Press.

Cooke, Philip (ed.) (2007), *Creative Regions: Technology and Culture,* Routledge, London.

Cox, George (2005), *Review on Creativity in Business,* HMSO, London, <http://www.hm-treasury.gov. uk/independent_reviews/cox_review/ coxreview_index>.

Cunningham, Stuart (2006), *What Price a Creative Economy?,* Platform Papers, no. 9, Currency House.

Currid, Elizabeth (2007), *The Warhol Economy: How Fashion, Art and Music Drive New York City,* Princeton University Press, Princeton.

Dawkins, Richard (1989), *The Selfish Gene,* Oxford University Press, Oxford.

Department for Culture, Media and Sport (2008), *The World's Creative Hub,* HMSO, London.

Diamond, Jared (2006), *Collapse: How Societies Choose to Fail or Survive,* Penguin.

Dubos, Rene (1980), *The Wooing of Earth,* Scribner's, New York.

Florida, Richard (2008), *Who's Your City?,* Basic Books, New York.

Florida, Richard (2001), *The Rise of the Creative Class,* Basic Books, New York.

Freeman, Alan, 'Is creation an industry?' *Creative Industry Journal.*

Frey, Bruno (2005), *What Values Should Count in the Arts? The Tension between Economic Effects and Cultural Value,* Institute for Empirical Research in Economics, University of Zurich.

Hall, Peter (2001), *Cities in Civilisation,* Fromm.

Hardin, Garrett (1968), 'The tragedy of the commons', *Science,* 162.

Hartley, John (ed.) (2005), *Creative Industries,* Blackwell, Oxford.

Heeks, Alan (2000), *The Natural Advantage: Renewing Yourself,* Nicholas Brealey, London.

Higgs, P. & Stuart Cunningham (2007), *Australia's Creative Economy: Mapping Methodologies,* ARC Centre of Excellence for Creative Industries and Innovation, QUT, Brisbane.

Howkins, John (2006), 'Why Michael Porter is wrong', *Australian Financial Review,* September.

Howkins, John (2001), *The Creative Economy,* Penguin.

Howkins, John & Zhao Li (2008), 'Dutty's Dare' ['遭遇创意队'], Xue Lin.

Hutton, Will (2007), *The Guardian,* 6 July.

Isaacs, William (1999), *Dialogue and the Art of Thinking Together,* Double-day, New York.

Jacobs, Jane (1985), *Cities and the Wealth of Nations,* Viking, New York.

Jensen, Rolf (2001), *The Dream Society,* McGraw-Hill, London.

Jouvenel, Bertrand (1981), *The Art of Conjecture,* Weidenfeld & Nicolson, New York.

Keane, Michael (2007), *Created in China: The Great New Leap Forward,* Routledge, London.

Keller, Evelyn Fox & Elizabeth A. Lloyd (1992), *Keywords in Evolutionary Biology,* Harvard University Press, Cambridge.

Kern European Affairs (KEA) (2006), *The Economy of Culture in Europe,* KEA.

Kingsland, Sharon (2005), *The Evolution of American Ecology* 1890-2000, John Hopkins University Press.

Kropotkin, Peter (1972), *Mutual Aid,* Allen Lane, London.

Kunzmann, Klaus (2004), 'Culture, Creativity and Spatial Planning', Abercrombie Lecture, University of Liverpool.

Leadbeater, Charles (2008), *We-Think: The Power of Mass Creativity,* Profile Books, London, <www.wethinkthebook.nei>.

Levin, Rick, and others (2000), *The ClueTrain Manifesto,* Perseus.

Lewin, Roger & Birsute Regine (2001), *Weaving Complexity and Business: Engaging the Soul at Work,* Texere.

Lovelock, James (2006), *The Revenge of Gaia,* Penguin.

Lunn, Peter (2008), *Basic Instinct: Human Nature and the New Economics,* Marshall Cavendish.

Macy, Joanna (1991), *Mutual Causality in Buddhism and General Systems Theory: The Dharma of Natural System,* State University of New York Press.

Naydler, Jeremy (ed.) (1996), *Goethe on Science,* Floris Books.

Nelson, Richard & Sidney Winter (1982), *Evolutionary Theory of Economic Change,* Harvard University Press.

NESTA (2006), *Creating Growth: How the UK Can Develop World Class Creative Businesses,* NESTA, London.

Nightingale, John & Jason Potts (2001), 'An alternative framework for economies', *Post-Autistic Economics Review,* no. 10, December.

Pine, Joseph & James Gilmore (1999), *The Experience Economy,* Harvard Business School, Boston.

Pinker, Steven (1999), *How the Mind Works,* Penguin.

Polenske, Karen (2007), *The Economic Geography of Innovation,* Cambridge University Press, Cambridge.

Potts, Jason (2007), 'Why the creative industries matter to economic evolution', STOREP-Brisbane Club: *Innovation and Complexity,* Pollenzo.

Schumpeter, Joseph (1949), *Theory of Economic Development,* Harvard University Press.

Schumpeter, Joseph (1943), *Capitalism, Socialism and Democracy,* Allen & Unwin, London.

Stoneman, P. (2007), An *introduction to the Definition and Measurement of Soft Innovation,* NESTA, London.

Tapscott, Don (2007), *Wikinomics,* Atlantic Books.

Tims, Charlie & Shelagh Wright (2007), *So, What Do You Actually Do?,* DEMOS, London.

Trinca, Helen & Catherine Fox (2004), *Better than Sex: How a Whole Generation Got Hooked on Work,* Random House.

UNCTAD (2008), *Creative Economy Report 2008,* UNCTAD.

Veblen, Thorstein (1899, 2007), *The Theory of the Leisure Class,* Oxford University Press.

Vul, Edward & Harold Pashler (2008), *The Crowd Within,* Department of Brain and Cognitive Science, MIT.

E.O. Wilson (1975), *Sociobiology,* Harvard University Press, Cambridge.

Wolf, Michael (1999), *The Entertainment Economy,* Times Books, New York.

Work Foundation (2007), *Staying Ahead: The Economic Performance of the UK's Creative Industries,* Work Foundation.

Worster, Donald (1994), *Nature's Economy: A History of Ecological Ideas,* Cambridge University Press, Cambridge.

Yarnit, Martin (ed.) (2007), *Advancing Opportunity: New Models of Schooling,* Smith Institute, United Kingdom.

Acknowledgements

This book has its roots in the discussions about the creative industries that started in Britain in the mid-1990s and
the many attempts since then to map, understand, improve
and strengthen this small but important slice of the national economy. I say 'national', but the British campaign
ignited similar discussions around the world, all wanting
to use creativity and innovation to bolster their cultural and
economic resources. We asked: What exactly is creativity?
What is the creative economy? What are the principles?
What are the rules? It soon became clear that the nature
of creativity is hard to explain and, of course, there are no
rules. There is, however, a substantial body of evidence and
some good policy tool-kits. There are too many people to
thank individually, but I want to mention my colleagues at
BOP Consulting, especially Jo Burns and Paul Owens, and
John Hartley, Stuart Cunningham and Brian Fitzgerald at
Queensland University of Technology.

The book is an attempt to put the creative economies in a

new context, and therefore my second source has been new thinking in neuro-science, education, urban design and business management, and emergent thinking in network and systems theory and the arts. My work on the Adelphi Charter on Creativity, Innovation and Intellectual Property enabled me to meet an extraordinary range of people (to whom many thanks), as did my research into business studies and ecology. I want to give special thanks to Ariane Bankes and Bronac Ferran and to Janine Edge and the Beacon Cottage Library.

The most direct source is a research project on creative ecologies carried out by the Shanghai School of Creativity for the Chinese government, for which I was asked to provide a global overview. I took the opportunity to tell the story from the beginning. But where to start? The date moved from the 1990s back to the 1960s, the postwar 1945 consensus, the Industrial Revolution, the Enlightenment, the Renaissance; and that was just in Europe. What about America? What about China? India? Brazil? Working in China encourages one to take a long view of history, in contrast to Americans whose memory seems shrivelled (remember the New Yorker who proclaimed the end of history in 1993?).[1] The Shanghai project was a marvellous opportunity to compare the West's creative ecology with China's. My report became the foundation of this book. I want to thank Li Wuwei, He Shougang, Zong Yu, Pan Jin and Guo Meijun in Shanghai; Su Tong and his colleagues in Beijing; Zhao Li in Shenzhen; Michael Keane; and my associate Chen Xu.

The fourth source is my own personal experience. Anyone writing about creativity draws on their own experience, openly or not, and I have used my experiences in magazine journalism, TV and film and my personal interest in contemporary art and photography. Creative people are notoriously uninterested in explaining the theory of what they are doing, and academics are often baffled by reality's failure to deliver the goods, but my personal pleasure and business success come together in the creative ecology, and whenever they diverge I want to know why.

Index